AF323038

CLASS AND CLASS CONFLICT IN POST-SOCIALIST CHINA

CLASS AND CLASS CONFLICT IN POST-SOCIALIST CHINA

Alvin Y So

Hong Kong University of Science and Technology, Hong Kong

NEW JERSEY · LONDON · SINGAPORE · BEIJING · SHANGHAI · HONG KONG · TAIPEI · CHENNAI

Published by

World Scientific Publishing Co. Pte. Ltd.

5 Toh Tuck Link, Singapore 596224

USA office: 27 Warren Street, Suite 401-402, Hackensack, NJ 07601

UK office: 57 Shelton Street, Covent Garden, London WC2H 9HE

Library of Congress Cataloging-in-Publication Data
So, Alvin Y., 1953–
   Class and class conflict in post-socialist China / by Alvin Y. So (Hong Kong University of Science and Technology, Hong Kong).
     pages cm
   Includes bibliographical references and index.
   ISBN 978-9814449649 (hardcover : alk. paper)
   1. Social classes--China--History. 2. Social conflict--China--History. 3. China--Social conditions--1949– I. Title.
   HN740.Z9S64633 2013
   305.50951--dc23

                                                            2013009943

British Library Cataloguing-in-Publication Data
A catalogue record for this book is available from the British Library.

In-house Editor: Monica Lesmana

Typeset by Stallion Press
Email: enquiries@stallionpress.com

Printed in Singapore by World Scientific Printers.

*To **Judy, Alina, Nadia, and Andre***

PREFACE

Suppose there is a time machine that could take us back to socialist China during the Cultural Revolution. About 60 years ago, we observed a highly elaborate vocabulary of class that pervaded the everyday life of the entire Chinese population. Every Chinese would carry a class label on his or her back, and one's social class label would play a prominent role in deciding who to make friends with, who to get married, what type of school you could be admitted to, what kind of job you could apply, whether you would be singled out as a target of attack in political campaigns, etc. During the mid 1960s–mid 1970s, you would not have been able to avoid hearing or reading the words "class" and "class conflict" if you had turned on a radio or TV, or read a newspaper or magazine anywhere on China.

However, about 30 years ago, the vocabulary of "class" and "class conflict" disappeared from the Chinese mass media, from the Chinese academic writings, and from everyday social life in the Chinese society. This disappearance was especially surprising given the fact that the mass media outside mainland China often reported that strikes, protests, petitions, demonstrations, and riots were happening all over China during the same period. I knew this fact first-hand because the Chinese translation of my paper on class and class conflict was prohibited from appearing in a book volume published in China.

It is this puzzle of the disappearance of the vocabulary of "class" and "class conflict" that prompted me to write a book on such a topic to explore the profound transformation of class and class conflict from socialist China to post-socialist China in the second half of the 20th century.

I would like to take this opportunity to express my sincere thanks for the support I have received in completing this book project. A grant from the Division of Social Science at HKUST has enabled me to do field work in the Pearl River Delta to study the migrant workers. A grant from HKUST-UCLA Collaborative Fund (co-PI with Ching Kwan Lee) enabled us to host two international conferences on "Class, Power, and China". I would also like to thank James Lee for his support for the two international conferences, and all the conference keynote speakers, presenters, discussants, and participants from Hong Kong, Taiwan, mainland China, and the U.S. for sharing their bright ideas on the issues of class and power in China.

Since several chapters are the revised version of my earlier papers published in *Critical Asian Studies*, *Journal of Contemporary Asia*, and Joseph Cheng's edited volumes, I sincerely thank the journal editors, Joseph Cheng, and the anonymous reviewers for their critical comments. Two chapters are drawn from the co-authored papers I wrote with Cindy Chu and Parry Leung. I therefore want to thank them for allowing me to use these two co-authored papers in this book.

In addition, I have benefited enormously from reading the works of many first-rate researchers on Chinese class and class conflict, among them Joel Andreas, Chris Chan, Cai Yongshun, Debby Davis, Ding Xueliang, David Goodman, Martin Hart-Landsberg, Richard Kraus, C.K. Lee, Pun Ngai, Mark Selden, Andy Walder, David Zweig, and the many others I cite in the reference section. Their studies have provided numerous insights and pertinent information, and my book has benefited from them.

Finally, I want to express sincere gratitude to my wife, Judy Chan So, and to my three loving children — Alina, Nadia, and Andre. They have sustained me unfaltering over the course of this book project, especially during the late 2000s when I had a minor stroke and a heart attack. Without their support and understanding, I doubt very much whether this book could have ever be completed.

CONTENTS

LIST OF TABLES

Chapter 1

INTRODUCTION

THE RESEARCH PROBLEM

In May 2010, four strike incidents were reported in Honda's production plants in China. The strike in Honda Auto Parts Manufacturing in Foshan, Guangdong province, involved over 1,800 workers and surprisingly lasted for 17 days. In the end, the workers won by getting a 32% increase in wages (from 1,544 yuan to 2,044 yuan). Since most strikes only last from half-a-day to a few days and are usually much less organized, the Honda Strike is considered quite extraordinary by Chinese standards.

What was especially significant about the Honda strike was the strikers not only raised their demands from higher wages to forming an independent trade union during the strike, but the strikers were also reported to have a physical confrontation with ACFTU (the official union supported by the communist party-state). Honda strikers reported they were beaten up by about 200 people mobilized by the town- and district-level trade unions. A few Honda strikers were hurt and sent to a nearby hospital (Chan and Hui, 2012).

Friedman (2012) described the Honda Strike as a turning point in Chinese labor politics because a momentous strike wave soon spread across factories, across industries, and even across regions in the summer of 2010 (Lau and Choi, 2010). Chinese workers are no longer satisfied with their defensive struggles (like making sure they are paid on time and getting back their wages owed by their employers). They are now fighting for higher wages, humane working conditions, and election of union officials, which are increasingly through direct and, at times, violent confrontation. This new wave of militant labor insurgency prompts the labor activists to predict that China will become the epicenter of global labor struggles (Litzinger, 2013; Friedman, 2012).

In June 2010, migrant workers in Zengcheng in Guangdong torched government offices after city security personnel pushed to the ground a pregnant migrant worker who had been working as a street vendor there. In September 2010, hundreds of peasants in Lufeng, also in Guangdong, participated in violent protests over the alleged seizure of villagers' land for development (Orlik, 2011).

Peasant protests also erupted in Wukan village in Guangdong when peasants became suspicious that the local government was in the process of selling land to County Gardens — a company which builds residency for the rich. Later, hundreds of peasants gathered at a nearby Communist Party office to nonviolently protest against the land sale. But as crowds grew and grew in numbers, so too did their confidence. Protesters began blocking roads and attacking buildings in a nearby industrial park. Three villagers were arrested at the Communist Party office demonstration, and the next day hundreds laid siege to the police station, demanding their release. The state responded to this challenge with unrestrained ferocity, with police and mercenaries beating villagers apparently without discrimination — men and women, children and the elderly. Cops were eventually called back to their posts, and the government struck a conciliatory tone, even asking villagers to elect delegates who could air their grievances. In retrospect, this seems to have been a ploy to uncover the "leadership" of the protesters. One of them — respected village butcher Xue Jinbo — died in police custody, apparently the victim of a state killing.

What happened next stunned Beijing authorities, and sent shockwaves around the world in mid-December 2011. The furious Wukan villagers banded together and drove the police and communist party officials out of town. They then set about running things for themselves. Meanwhile, cops maintained a blockade a few miles away. After Wukan villagers received enormous support from nearby villagers in Guangdong and from the international mass media, the communist leadership decided to cut a deal. Though details are scarce and unreliable, the provincial government reportedly agreed to buy land it had seized, and an investigation into the death of Xue Jinbao was announced. More importantly, Wukan peasant delegates would be allowed to stand in local elections and elect their own village government (Django, 2012).

Aside from the above well-known worker strike in Honda and the peasant protest in Wukan, numerous social protests have also been reported in China at the turn of the 21st century. Murray Tanner (2005) reports that social protest has risen dramatically over the past decade and is now a daily phenomenon in China's political system. In the Ministry of Public Security (MPS) report of "mass group incident" (*quntixing shijian*) — an overly broad catch-all term that encompasses the full spectrum of group protests — including sit-ins, strikes, group petitions, rallies, demonstrations, marches, traffic-blocking and building seizures, and even some public melees, riots, and inter-ethnic strife — the number of "mass incidents" has skyrocketed from about 8,700 in 1993, to about 10,000 in 1994, to about 50,000 in 2002, to about 58,000 in 2003, to about 60,000 in 2006, to about 80,000 in 2007, to 127,000 in 2008, to 180,000 in 2010, and to more than 200,000 in 2011 (Feng, 2012; Hui and Chan, 2011; Tanner, 2005; Page, 2011; Roberts and Zhao, 2011).

In response, the Chinese communist party-state reportedly, in 2011, spent more on internal security (US\$111 billion) than on national defense (US\$106 billion). The costs of making the "harmonious society", as current party-leader called it, are indeed very high. Yet there are real questions over whether the current approach is sustainable (Gobel and Ong, 2012, p. 7).

The insurgency of class conflict in Chinese society was finally reflected in the conflict within the communist party. In March 2012, the notions of stability and consensus in China's secretive political system took a possibly big hit by the dismissal of Bo Xilai, the Party Secretary of metropolitan Chongqing. Mr. Bo is mostly identified as the charismatic leader of China's new left by the intellectuals and policy wonks who argue that China should use state power to assure social equality and enforce a culture of moral purity and nationalism. Mr. Bo's policies in Chongqing, from the mass singing of Mao-era songs to his pitiless anti-corruption campaign, had earned him strong support from the citizens of Chongqing (Wines, 2012).

As Zhao (2012, p. 1) points out, Bo was no ordinary Politburo member of the Chinese Communist Party, and his Chongqing model was not just another instance of "decentralized experimentation" so characteristic of the communist policy-making process. What was increasingly at issue, and was emphasized by the press, was the contrast between the two models of development: the "Guangdong Model" which symbolized a more free market approach, rising inequality, and export orientation, and the "Chongqing Model" which was characterized as looking to revitalize socialist ideas and populist claims in its push for rapid and balanced development. At stake today, then, is not just the fate of Bo, but also China's revolutionary past, the complicated intersections of socialist and capitalist class politics, and the unfinished struggle for socialism in China.

The downfall of Mr. Bo coincided with the publication of a World Bank (2012) report entitled *China 2030: Building a Modern, Harmonious, and Creative High-Income Society*. The World Bank report advocated the breaking up of state-owned enterprises (SOEs), increasing private competition, and liberalizing the finance sector. That the World Bank report was created in collaboration with the Development Research Center of the State Council indicates that it reflects deep and powerful interests in the Chinese economy, which call for renewed commitment to "market reform" in an attempt to shore up support for the Chinese government's neoliberal policies.

THE FRAMEWORK

Observing the rapid rise of mass incidents in China over the past two decades, Martin Hart-Landsberg and Paul Burkett (2004, p. 9) argue that "China's market reforms have led not to socialist renewal but rather to full-fledged capitalist restoration, including foreign economic domination". In addition, they show that this pro-market transition is highly costly, leading to rising unemployment, economic insecurity, inequality, intensified exploitation, declining health and education conditions, exploding government debt, and unstable prices. Consequently, they conclude, the progressive community in the West is wrong to celebrate China as an economic success story. Further, they insist that researchers have to bring Marxism back in so as to provide the "theoretical clarity and strategic perspective necessary to help us transform the world" (Landsberg and Burkett, 2004, p. 24).

Similarly, Bruce Boon (2006) argues that China's headlong drive towards neoliberal capitalism is beginning to meet resistance. Lemos (2012) reported that the Chinese people had lost their optimism and were yearning for security. Income is a primary source of worry for those who have lost their jobs or land. Pensions and social welfare payments are almost nonexistent. People struggle to pay for education. They cannot afford medical treatment; clinics and hospitals require patients to pay cash in advance. A serious illness can spell financial ruin for an entire family.

Moreover, workers' protests are growing. Opposition is being voiced within the rank of the Chinese Communist Party itself. Boon predicts that it is a merely a matter of time before the class struggle erupts on a grand scale. With the deepening of revisionist clique's push for privatization, class contradictions in China are bound to become more acute; and the masses will certainly intensify their struggles on ever wider scales. Boon further predicts that when development of contradictions and mass struggles nationwide reach a climax, the people within the Party, the government and the army who have understood the true nature of revisionism will wage a resolute struggle against it, and will rejoin the proletarian class ranks to hold high the banner of Mao Zedong and to resume their fight for socialism in China.

The Marxist analysis of Hart-Landsberg/Burkett and Boon, however, are derived mostly from the polarization model presented in Marx's *Capital.* If capitalism has been restored in China, then the logic of capital and the polarization model should be applicable. In the editors' foreword to Hart-Landsberg and Burkett's special issue on China and Socialism, Magdoff and Foster (2004, p. 4) further spell out the assumption underlying this *polarization model:* "Under capitalism, driven by profit for the few, accumulation occurs on a world scale while the great majority of the world's masses are plunged into misery. And, as shown by Hart-Landsberg and Burkett, the Chinese case is a witness to the fact that growth with the purpose of increasing profits, or growth merely for the sake of growth, leads inevitably to stark social inequality". This polarization model in *Capital* postulates that the antagonism between capital and labor in production is basic to the understanding of the historical development of capitalism. And it further predicts that the structural contradiction in capitalism would lead to simplification of class antagonism, with the concentration of ownership in the hands of the capitalist class, on the one hand, and the proletarianization and the increasing misery of the working class, on the other. Society as a whole is splitting more and more into two great hostile camps, into two great classes directly facing each other (So and Suwarsono, 1990).

Hart-Landsberg and Burkett's contribution is the application of *Capital*'s polarization model to the Chinese context. Although this exercise helps to illuminate the growing capital/labor contradiction in China, it has misread the class situation in China because it assumes that the Chinese society is so polarized with class conflict that the communist party-state will soon collapse, like other Eastern European communist regimes in their post-socialist transition.

In addition, the structural contradiction of capital and labor in production relations, upon which Hart-Landsberg and Burkett based their argument, is discussed at a high level of abstraction and is taken to be universally applicable to every capitalist society. What is overlooked in this mode of analysis, however, is historical specificity, i.e., how the logic of capital actually works itself out in a concrete historical setting and is embedded with specific national traits. In the Chinese historical context, for example, market reforms emerged in a context in which the communist party-state directly controlled almost every aspect of the economy and society. Thus, it is crucial to bring the communist party-state back in to examine the capitalist turn in post-socialist China.

Furthermore, based as it is on the logic of capital and focused on capital/labor relationship, Hart-Landsberg and Burkett's structural analysis tends to be economistic. Their focus is on workers' exploitation, overproduction, and class struggle on the economic front. Other factors such as the state and state–society relations are barely taken into consideration. I argue that this economistic polarization model is inadequate and too simplified to provide a comprehensive picture of China's historical development. In what follows, I offer an analysis that highlights the role of the state and the interaction between the state and social classes.

While the Marxist literature has over-stressed the salience of class in presenting a polarization model to analyze China, the academic literature on mainland China, on the other hand, has been completely silent on the issues concerning class and class conflict. Pun Ngai and Chris Chan (2008) report that there is the subsumption of class discourse in China. The language of class is subsumed so as to clear the way for a neoliberal economic discourse that emphasizes individualism, professionalism, equal opportunities, and the open market. Yingjie Guo (2009) also points out that the Chinese academia has discarded the concept of class; class analysis is replaced by "stratum analysis"; and "relation of conflict are bypassed in the construction while antagonism is defined out of stratum".

The literature about China similarly offers a stratification analysis of the impact of marketization on the Chinese society. The debate between the "market transition" theorists and the so-called "state-centered" theorists is on whether the power of state managers has been eroded by market forces, whether inequalities have increased in the market transition after 1978, and whether human capital, social network, entrepreneurship, and the local state have induced new forms of inequality as economic reforms progressed. This market transition debate has clarified our understanding of the intricate linkages between market, inequalities, and social strata in the post-reform era, and has made a significant contribution to the literature of social stratification and Chinese society (Nee, 1989, Parish and Michelson, 1996; Walder, 1996).

Nevertheless, except for a couple of researchers, the literature on socialist market transition has so far avoided raising the issues of classes and class conflict in its analysis. This negligence of class analysis in the China field is unfortunate because class analysis has proved to be an important method in historical and comparative sociology. The works of E. P. Thompson (1978), Barrington Moore (1966), and I. Wallerstein (1984) have used class analysis to make sense of the origins of democracy and dictatorship and the transformation from feudalism to capitalism.

In this historical perspective, class is conceptualized as a historical process: a dynamics process of perpetual re-creation and hence of constant change in form and composition. As Wallerstein (1979, p. 224) points out, "classes do not have some permanent reality. Rather, they are formed, they consolidate themselves, they disintegrate or disaggregate, and they are reformed. It is a process of constant movement, and the greatest barrier to understanding their action is reification".

The aim of class analysis is to trace how classes emerged and transformed in a certain historical period. Furthermore, class is not an attribute but is always a set of changing relationships with other classes in a certain historical contact (Wallerstein, 1979, p. 224). Similarly, Thompson (1978) formulates class as a historical relationship: "Class, in the Marxist tradition, is (or ought to be) a *historical category*, describing *people in relationship over time* and the way in which they become conscious of their relationships, separate, unite, enter into struggle, form institutions and transmit values in class ways" (italics in original). Class analysis is thus aimed to examine the dynamic relationship among classes and between classes and the state. Class cannot be examined when isolated from one another (So and Hikam, 1989).

RESEARCH QUESTIONS AND KEY ARGUMENTS

Using the lens of a historical class analysis, this book poses the following three sets of research questions: (1) *The Emergence Questions*: How were the old social classes in China destroyed or remade during the socialist transformation in the Maoist era (1949–1978)? After China decided to move towards neoliberal capitalist, what state policies have led to the re-emergence of classes and what is the new pattern of class conflict in the post-socialist era since 1978? (2) *The Character Question*: What is the distinctive pattern of class and class conflict in post-socialist China? In what ways are the classes in post-socialist China different from the classes in other social formation? (3) *The Agency Questions*: Could social classes in China become historical agents of structural change? Could social classes and class conflict lead to a regime change, or a proletarian revolution, or a bourgeois revolution in China in the near future?

In brief, the main argument of the book is that during the socialist era (1949–1978), China built an all-powerful communist party-state to carry out all sorts of revolutionary policies for socialist construction. The communist party-state not only had abolished private property, but also had undermined the socio-political bases of the capitalist class and the landlord class. However, socialist China was far from an ideal equalitarian society. Although China succeeded in overthrowing the old ruling class and cut down the old class inequality, new class inequalities and *a new class* nevertheless emerged during the socialist construction through which a foundation was laid for the numerous "class struggles" during the Cultural Revolution.

Although new classes and new class relationships have emerged from the market reforms launched in 1978, the Communist Party still holds a political monopoly, and the state is still a developmental one and has continued to play a decisive role in reconstructing the contours of class formation and class conflict (Szelenyi, 2008). Its strong influence in the developmental process has created a hybrid *state neoliberal capitalism* model; the close linkage between the public and the private sectors has created a hybrid *cadre-capitalist class*; its former institutions in the socialist era (household registration and work unit) have divided the working class. Its bifurcated structure has shaped the pattern of class conflict of both the working class and the peasantry; and its fusion with new middle class professionals has prompted them toward the path of *quiet democratization*.

This book is divided into two parts. The first two chapters in Part I will sketch the key developmental policies and the crucial historical events in socialist China and in post-socialist China. These two chapters are aimed to introduce the historical setting to help readers understand the changing contour of class and class conflict from 1949 to the present.

Using a historical approach, the five chapters in Part II are aimed to trace the making and the remaking of various social classes, namely, the capitalist class, the old urban working class, the new migrant working class, the peasantry, and the new middle class during the socialist and the post-socialist transformation. Each chapter will examine the distinctive characteristics, the pattern of class conflict with the party-state and other social classes, and the potential that this class will become an agent of historical transformation and structural change in post-socialist China. Toward the end, there is a Conclusion chapter to summarize the key arguments presented in this book as well as to discuss whether post-socialist China is moving toward a capitalist democracy, or a proletarian/peasant class revolution.

Chapter 2

CLASS AND CLASS CONFLICT IN SOCIALIST CHINA (1949–1978)

CLASS AND CLASS CONFLICT IN PRE-1949 CHINA

Although the Chinese communist party (CCP) characterized the Chinese pre-revolutionary social order as "feudal" or "semi-feudal", the use of the term *feudalism* is highly misleading in imperial China because there were few legal impediments to social and geographical mobility (Watson, 1984, p. 2; Whyte, 2010, p. 14). While Chinese rural landlords owed their ability to live privileged lives to their ownership of a disproportionate share of village land, they had no special legal status granted by the imperial bureaucracy, and their neighbors who managed to amass a similar amount of land could be transformed similarly from peasant into landlord. Still, there was a symbiosis between the landlord class and the imperial bureaucracy. Barrington Moore (1966, p. 170) explains that "landed wealth came out of the bureaucracy and depended on the bureaucracy for its existence". The imperial bureaucracy constituted an alternative way of squeezing an economic surplus out of the peasants. In addition, the imperial bureaucracy's system of examinations and Confucian doctrines enhanced the legitimacy and the superior social status of the landlord class as long as some member of the landlord's family, or an adopted bright youngster, could manage to acquire an academic degree and pass an imperial examination.

Nevertheless, the incorporation of China into the capitalist world-economy has led to the breaking up of the imperial state in

11

the early 20th century, the symbiosis between the landlord class and the imperial state was broken, giving rise to new forms of class conflict in the Chinese society. In the countryside, as the prestigious landed upper class was de-legitimized to "evil gentry" and local bullies, landless poor peasants were forced to engage in a desperate struggle in order to survive. In the urban areas, as China started the first wave of industrialization in the coastal cities, the nascent working class began to form unions, organize strikes, and engage in bread-and-butter struggles with the Chinese and foreign capitalists. Nevertheless, there were no more than 1 million industrial workers in a land of 400 million people (Meisner, 1999, p. 6); the nascent workers retained strong ties to their native villages and to the peasant tradition and failed to develop a modern sense of proletarian class consciousness. The new middle class intellectuals at first initiated a modest path towards reforms and democracy, but they were soon pushed to the side of peasants and workers as class conflict intensified. Of course, class conflict, by itself, is insufficient to start a revolution. However, class conflict had laid the foundation of the communist revolution when the CCP seized the gold opportunity to wage political struggles against the ruling Nationalist government and the Japanese invaders during World War II.

THE COMMUNIST REVOLUTION AND THE FORCED WITHDRAWAL FROM THE CAPITALIST WORLD-ECONOMY

The immediate reaction of the capitalist states towards the 1949 Chinese Communist Revolution was to suppress it through military intervention. The capitalist states were concerned that the winds of communism would spread quickly to other states in East Asia. During the Cold War, the United States took an active role in attempting to destroy the new socialist state in China: it sent warships to patrol the Taiwan Strait and supported the defeated Nationalist Party in Taiwan, sent soldiers to fight against the communists in Korea, supported counter-revolutionaries activities in China, froze Chinese assets in the United States, prevented China from gaining a seat in the United Nations, imposed an economic embargo against China, and waged ideological attacks on Chinese "communist totalitarianism" in the mass media.

Facing such hostilities from the capitalist states, socialist China had no choice but to withdraw from the capitalist world-economy. After the 1949 Communist Revolution, the CCP was forced to sever diplomatic relations with the West due to core hostilities. Political isolation was then followed by economic isolation. Socialist China's foreign trade with the West came almost to a halt due to the U.S. embargo, and it could not rely on foreign capital investment either, as most foreign capitalists had already left by the time of the Korean War in the early 1950s. Cutting off from contacts with the capitalist states, socialist China could not possibly pursue either export-led industrialization (due to the closure of Western markets) or import-substitution (due to economic embargo). Therefore, socialist China was forced to miss a golden opportunity for achieving economic development during the post World War II boom in the 1950s–1960s.

Richard Kraus (1979) points out that this forced withdrawal from the capitalist world-economy had produced an interesting contradiction in China: the more the United States heightened its hostilities toward China, the more the CCP was determined to move rapidly into socialism in order to consolidate its supports from the peasants and workers.

PRE-1956 DEVELOPMENTAL POLICIES AND THEIR CLASS TARGETS

The Korean War, the economic blockade by the United States, and the forced withdrawal from the world-economy in the 1950s had induced a strong communist party-state in China, because China's political order had to be strengthened to confront the "imperialist enemies" from without (notably during the Korean War) and the "counter-revolutionaries" from within (notably the remnants of the Nationalist Party opposition). Due to the fusion of functions and the overlapping of personnel among the communist party, the state bureaucracy, and the army, there was an excess concentration of power in the vanguard

Leninist Party. Only political organizations (like peasants' associations, labor unions, and women's associations) formally sponsored by the party were allowed to operate; other organizations were either made ineffective or simply banned from operation.

This Leninist party-state was all-powerful in the sense that it extended both vertically and horizontally to every sphere in the Chinese society. Vertically, the Leninist party-state was the first Chinese state that was able to exert its political power all the way down to village, family, and individual levels. Horizontally, there was a great expansion of state functions. The Leninist state did not just collect tax and keep social order, but also oversaw such functions as education, health care, marriage, culture, and carried out such developmental policies (like Land Reform and collectivization) and political movements (like the Cultural Revolution). In this respect, the Chinese communist party-state had even more state autonomy and more state capacity than its developmental state counterparts in Japan, South Korea, and Taiwan. Equipped with such a strong party-state, China was ready to carry out its radical equalitarian experiment during the 1950s and 1960s.

Intensive hostility from the United States has also induced the CCP to drop its moderate "**New Democracy Policy**". During World War II, the CCP presented itself as a nationalist party in order to unite all the Chinese (including the landlords and capitalists) to fight against Japanese invasion. In the so-called "New Democracy Policy", the CCP suggested that "a good many of the enlightened gentry who are middle and small landlords…and we should unite with them in the common fight against Japan" (Mao, 1967, pp. 319–320). The CCP also suggested that "the national bourgeoisie is a class with a dual character. On the one hand, it is oppressed by imperialism and fettered by feudalism and consequently is in contradiction with both of them. In this respect, it constitutes one of the revolutionary forces". (Mao, 1967, p. 320)

However, the CCP quickly dropped the New Democracy Policy in the early 1950s when it was forced to withdraw from the capitalist world-economy. In order to withstand foreign aggression, the CCP needed to consolidate its external and internal bases of support.

Externally, socialist China turned to the Soviet Union for help in spite of their policy differences in the 1930s (because the Soviet Union did not support a guerrilla warfare strategy). Internally, the CCP wanted to ensure the loyalty of its key supporters.

At the height of the Korean War, the CCP carried out **land reform** at full speed in order to consolidate support from the peasantry. Through violent confrontations with the landlords, the poor peasants gradually asserted themselves, acquired the political capacity to protect their class interests, and took land ownership away from the landlords. In this respect, the land reform was proclaimed to be a great success. Not only did it satisfy the land hunger of the poor peasants, it also politically mobilized the peasantry as a class and consolidated the power of the CCP in the countryside.

However, giving land to the peasantry was not a sufficient mean to bring social equality to the countryside. Large peasant families, because they possessed more labor power, were allocated more farmland, more farm instruments, and more farm animals than the small peasant families. Consequently, shortly after the completion of land reform, rapid class differentiation in the Chinese countryside was seen. Large peasant families were getting richer, while small peasants were falling further behind in their socioeconomic status.

In response to this growing class differentiation, the CCP put forward **collectivization** policies. Farmland and other resources became collectively owned, and peasants, from large and small families alike, worked collectively in agricultural cooperatives. Rewards were distributed according to peasant's contributions to labor and to farm instruments. This collectivization policy was aimed at stopping class differentiation within the countryside, thereby eliminating the rich peasant stratum, and imposing restrictions on rural markets. Collectivization also extends the reach of the state to the individual peasant, making possible extraction of a larger share of agricultural surplus, substantial portions of which were transferred to industry and cities through compulsory sales to the state at low fixed prices of collectively produced grain and cotton.

Meanwhile, in the cities, the CCP began to nationalize its industries. The **nationalization** drive was made easier because considerable number of Chinese or foreign wealthy capitalists had already fled to Hong Kong and Taiwan in 1949 and for the most part their enterprises and other property were nationalized and run by the state in the early 1950s (Whyte, 2010, p. 16). Although nationalization was aimed at eliminating the capitalist as a class, the CCP wanted to minimize the dissatisfaction of the "national capitalists" because it depended on their management skills and technical expertise to run the urban economy. As a result, the CCP not only paid compensation to the capitalists for their industrial assets, it also hired them as directors to manage the factories. After nationalization, the state dominated the urban economy and central planning was made possible.

The advent of socialism and central planning during 1955–1957 made it possible for the party-state to initiate their control over job assignments and labor mobility, with new employees assigned to a firm rather than hired through a process of competition in the labor market. Wage payments for the urban workers were henceforth set by the party-state, rather than being based on labor market competition and the capitalist's discretion. Socialist China provided what became known as an "iron rice bowl" — secure employment and wages combined with a wide range of fringe benefits that workers in Western advanced industrial countries could only envy. This "iron rice bowl" employment relationship enabled the CCP to secure support of the urban working class.

Once the capitalist class was eliminated, the next target of the CCP was the new middle class. In the mid-1950s, Western-trained Chinese intellectuals, who believed in the ideals of bourgeois democracy and individualism, became more and more critical to the new policies of the socialist state. They conveyed negative feelings toward the CCP and wanted to form a second political party during the **Hundred Flowers Campaign** in 1957. In this withdrawal phase, the CCP could not afford the luxury of tolerating an internal dissent group, for this would weaken national unity and give the United

States an excuse to intensify its hostilities toward China. Thus, the CCP quickly cracked down on the dissenting intellectuals — they were labeled as "rightists"; they were not allowed to publish their writings or make public appearances; and many were banished to remote regions to carry out "thought reform". Through this ideological hegemony, the CCP successfully mobilized the Chinese people to carry out its radical socialist experiments.

In sum, hostilities from the capitalist states and withdrawal from the capitalist world-economy led China to pursue such radical developmental policies as land reform, collectivism, and nationalization. In order to arouse uninterrupted enthusiasm from the masses, the CCP put forward an egalitarian de-stratification experiment, eliminating the interests of all the property-based classes.

SOCIALIST TRANSFORMATION AND THE EMERGENCE OF NEW CLASS RELATIONS AFTER 1956

The year 1956 is often considered as the turning point in China's socialist development because socialist institutions were introduced on a wide scale in that year (Kraus, 1981, p. 12). In 1956, China's CCP leaders were united in an optimistic assessment of class conflict in their country. China had succeeded in overthrowing the old ruling class (the landlords and the capitalists), in casting out imperialist powers, in rebuilding a war-ravaged economy, in establishing an institutional basis for socialist construction, and in apparently forging a new unity among the Chinese people. All these factors contributed to a hopeful mood in which large-scale social conflict seemed less prominent.

The notion that the class issue had been largely resolved by the introduction of socialism contained a fundamental assumption about the Chinese revolution: the struggle had ended with liberation, land reform, collectivization and nationalization, when the former exploiters were deprived of their economic ownership and other privileges, and were relegated to inferior positions with respect to those whom they had formerly oppressed. Justice had been done, and the world had been righted. In addition, a massive program of industrialization had begun with Soviet advice, making China's economic prospects brighter than at any time in the 20th century. A civil service reform was under way as well, transforming old guerrilla fighters into modern administrators.

However, the notion that the class issue has been resolved seemed to be premature. Although the former ruling class had been destroyed and the old property-based class conflict had been diminished, new social inequalities were emerging in socialist China which could be intensified to class contradiction and class conflict. Feng Wang (2008, pp. 25–45) points to the following new categories (which emerged largely as a product of socialist China's planned economy): locale, ownership type, and work organization. These new categories served as the basis of economic organization, social control, and benefits distribution under socialism.

The first new category is **locale**. The separation between urban and rural China is one of the significant legacies of the Chinese socialism. In the process of China's socialist industrialization, the urban sector was privileged over the rural sector, though the latter accounted for up to 80% of China's population in the 1950s. Not only did China's industrialization rely heavily on the extraction of resources from the countryside and an exploitation of the peasants, but urban Chinese who were more centrally involved in industrial development received much better rewards. In order to promote industrialization as quickly as possible to catch up with the Western capitalist states, the party-state arbitrarily set low prices for agricultural products and high prices for industrial goods. Such a biased policy provided a basis for cheap raw materials, low cost for urban workers, and a high profit rate for industrial products. When the party-state realized that it could not provide the same benefits to the whole population, it enacted strict regulations (so-called the *hukou* system) to prevent migration from rural to urban area. Thus, the *hukou* **(household registration)** system serves to divide the population into a rural household status and an urban household status. On the basis of this differentiation, urban and rural Chinese were separated in terms of grain supply, supply of non-staple good and fuel, housing, education, employment, medical care, old-age support, labor insurance and protection, personnel policy, military conscription, marriage, and childbearing. In summary, rural and urban Chinese faced totally different life chances and class situation based on their residency. The dichotomy between rural and urban therefore went far beyond geographical or residential divisions; it was economic, social, and political (Wang, 2008, pp. 30–31).

The second new category is ***ownership type***. Ownership in pre-1978 socialist China was mainly along the lines of the state-owned and the collective-owned sectors. The state-owned sector in socialist China was the most privileged sector under the planned economy system. The state invested heavily in this sector, controlled capital and labor allocation, production, and distribution of profits, and provided better benefits for employees in this sector in comparison to other sectors. In 1970, it employed 75% of all urban workers and produced 87.6% of the gross industrial output. Collectively-owned units were nominally owned by their workers, and they received much less state investment and fewer benefits during the planned economy period. Collective enterprises were not as capital-intensive and were in the service and light industry sectors, and their wages and benefits in general also lagged behind those in the state sector (Wang, 2008, p. 32).

The third new category is **work organization (*danwei*)**. At the very basic level of society, urban Chinese were organized into *danwei*, or "work units". With the disappearance of private economy in urban China by the late 1950s, almost all urban Chinese were incorporated into work units. *Danwei* served as the employer, social welfare benefits distributor, and an arena for political mobilization and control (Walder, 1986; Lu and Perry, 1997). For example, work units provided 90% of the urban housing during the socialist era; more than 40% of state enterprises ran schools of some kind; and about 40% of all general hospital beds were in state-owned industrial systems. As shown by Lu and Perry (1997, p. 8), "the functions of *danwei* can be divided into two areas: political and social. These two functions may be characterized as 'paternalistic' and 'maternalistic' respectively. As in a traditional family, the *danwei* acts as a patriarch who disciplines and sanctions his children, while at the same time serving as a maternal provider of care and daily necessities".

Aside from the above new categories created during the process of socialist industrialization, there was also a concern on the emergence of **a new class** inside the party-state apparatus: a group of fat and contented bureaucrats, happy to enjoy the privileges of the society which they administrated.

In the years of revolutionary struggle before the victory of the revolution, the cadres of the communist movement were without a well-defined hierarchy of ranks. Remuneration for completed work followed the "supply system" in which cadres were provided with life's necessities in a rather egalitarian manner, with only three differentiated grades by which cadres were issued housing, food, etc.

The formal hierarchy of civil service ranks which was introduced along with the socialization drive in 1956 reflected the strong Soviet influence then present in China. Each state cadre was assigned to one of 30 grades (*jibie*) with grade 1 for the Chairman and Vice-Chairman of the state, and grade 26 for the lowliest cadre. Ranks 27 through 30 were reserved for janitorial and other service personnel. The formal hierarchy of civil service rank is important for providing markers of status and power as well as income differentiation. Rank is known within an organization, and is even evident outside through such manifestations as distinctions in dress, deportment, or access to automobiles.

During the high tide of socialization in 1956, there was a concern about the ease with which many cadres had detached themselves from the masses. The CCP had issued a directive which instructed leading cadres at all levels to participate in physical labor as "not a few comrades who were influenced by the thinking of the exploiting classes of the old society have now forgotten this excellent tradition and they look down upon physical labor. A concern for fame, advantage, and position is growing among them" (cited in Kraus, 1981, p. 65).

There is also a concern that special preparatory schools were expanded in the cities, where they catered to cadre children. On the other hand, the proportion of college students of worker or peasant background declined from 67% to 38% of the student body of Beijing University between 1958 to 1962 (Kraus, 1981, p. 69).

As socialist transformation had increased the need for officials to manage a state-controlled economy, the number of state cadres increased eightfold between 1949 and 1958. There was a worry that the revolutionary commitment of the party's member might be under-mined by the daily routine of administration, especially as the newly recruited cadres have not participated in the pre-1949 revolutionary struggle. This worry is perhaps more evident in an undated discussion of "Twenty Manifestations of Bureaucracy". Two samples from Mao's bitter catalog will reflect his concern for the rise of the new class:

> The bureaucratic attitude is immense; they cannot have any direction; they are egoistic; ... they cause people to become afraid just by looking at them; they repeatedly hurl all kinds of abuse at people...
>
> They seek pleasure and fear hardships; they engage in back door deals; one person becomes an official and the entire family benefits; one person reaches nirvana and all his close associates rise up to heaven; there are parties and gifts and presents... (Kraus, 1981, p. 74)

Mao's concern with the work methods of cadres led to a more general concern with privilege within the state bureaucracy.

> Some cadres now scramble for fame and fortune and are inter-ested only in personal gain... They vie with each other not in plain living, doing more work and having few comforts, but for luxuries, rank, and status. At present, this kind of thinking has grown con-siderably in the party and the matter demand our attention (Kraus, 1981, p. 75).

In sum, there are concerns that some of the state bureaucrats had emerged as a new exploiting class in socialist China. This new class enjoyed privileges such as high salaries, special housing recrea-tion homes, frequent vacation trips, and access to scarce resources such as special shops and Western consumer goods. Furthermore, this new class was in the process of passing these class privileges to their second generation.

In their discussion on durable inequalities and the legacy of revolution, Ching Kwan Lee and Mark Selden (2007) also point out that the revolutionary processes of land reform and collectivization had homogenized the complex social structure of pre-revolutionary rural China. On the one hand, property-based income inequality was eliminated, giving rise to a highly egalitarian intra-village income distribution. On the other hand, a two-class structure of collectivized peasants and cadres emerged with the latter exercising a monopoly of political power and they had access to scarce resources.

The cities too had experienced a homogenization of diverse classes into a two-class system of working people and officials (the cadres), while eradicating the extremes of wealth and status characteristics of pre-revolutionary China. Peasants and workers were beneficiaries of socialist transformation, the former through equalization of land ownership and income, the latter through the provision of secure employment with generous welfare provisions. However, since 1956, class differences in socialist China hinged neither on property nor the ownership of the means of production, but rather on the differential access to power through the party-state, which controlled both collectives and state-owned enterprises. How then did the socialist party-state respond to this emergent new class whose power is derived from the control of the party-state?

THE CHALLENGES OF THE NEW CLASS TO THE SOCIALIST PARTY-STATE

Even though the party-state waged class struggles against the landlords, the capitalists, and the intellectuals for over three decades, it never has experienced in waging a class struggle against its own members (cadres, state officials, and party leaders). The rise of the new class thus presented many new challenges for the party-state.

First of all, there was **the challenge of leadership** (or vanguard). Before 1956, the party-state acted as the leader (or the vanguard) of the class revolution. The party-state planned the strategy of class revolution, identified friends and enemies, mobilized the activists, aroused the enthusiasm of the masses, disciplined the free-riders, and legitimatized the activities of the revolution; afterwards, the party-state trained the movement activists into leaders of the class revolution and recruited them to the party-state.

However, in the 1960s, the party-state found itself the target of the class revolution; cadres and officials were accused of abusing their power and benefitting themselves at the expenses of workers and peasants. As such, which agent is going to act as the leader (or the vanguard) to plan, organize, mobilize, and legitimatize the class revolution in socialist China after 1956?

In addition, there was **the challenge of class**. Which definition should be used to define class in socialist China? Before the socialist transformation in 1956, property or ownership of the means of production was used to identify the exploiters (the landlords and the capitalists). Owners of the means of production, due to the fact that they have the power to exclude non-owners from the production process, were able to extract a larger share of surplus over the non-owners, and thus were able to enjoy a much higher living standard than the non-owners.

After 1956, however, this **property-based definition** of class was outdated because it was no longer useful to identify different classes (owners from non-owners) in socialist China. After nationalization and collectivization, ownership took the form of state ownership or collective ownership, while private ownership was strongly suppressed or eliminated. Former owners (like landlords and capitalists) could no longer exploit the peasants and workers by taking a larger share of surplus from the production process.

As such, which criteria should be used to define class in socialist China after 1956? Since the property-based definition was no longer useful, the Leftist Red Guards in the Cultural Revolution used a **power-based definition** to define class in order to attack the emergent new class in the party-state. The party-state has evolved into a new ruling class and has developed its own interests that are antagonistic to the interests of the peasants and workers (Wortzel, 1987).

It is the control of the state apparatus, not the control of the means of production, which defines the new class in socialist China. Thus, the power holder in the party-state is said to be the new ruling class or the "capitalist". The new class is characterized by its extraction of surplus from the state machinery (either legally or illegally through corruption), enabling the new class to get access to special resources and life chances, to live an extravagant life style that is distinguished from the masses, and to pass its class privileges to its offsprings. Thus, bureaucrats themselves form a class, with interests sharply antagonistic to those of the workers and peasants.

The above power-based definition, however, would condemn the entire bureaucratic elites in the party-state, label *all* of them as members of the new class and would disqualify them as the supporters of the socialist revolution. The implication of such definition is that all the existing state officials should be dismissed. This power-based definition is based on the anarchy assumption that you cannot trust anybody in power and you have to smash the entire party-state apparatus to continue the socialist revolution. Adopting such power-based definition would be suicidal for the CCP as it would alienate many of the officials whose interests it sought to identify and would also deprive the party-state from getting any supports of the existing bureaucrats. Even at the height of the Cultural Revolution, the Maoist leadership had insisted upon differentiating among cadres to locate 95% who were good or basically good (Kraus, 1981, p. 149).

Obviously, the CCP would need to design a new definition of class in order to distinguish the good cadres from the bad cadres in the state apparatus.

TOWARD A NEW CONCEPTION OF CLASS IN POST-1956 SOCIALIST CHINA

In the Western capitalist states, class is a useful analytical tool to understand social conflicts and social changes in capitalist societies. Class analysis helps to locate the structural cleavages in a society; it helps to trace source of conflict; it identifies the agents who are induced to change the existing economic, social, and political structure, the agents who could serve as alliance, and the agents who should be identified as adversaries of revolution.

Before 1956, the CCP employed Lenin's definition of class which emphasizes structural location and conflict in the production sphere (Kraus, 1981, p. 21):

> Classes are large group of people which differ from each other by the place they occupy in a historically determined system of social production, by their relation to the means of production, by their role in the social organization of labor, and consequently, by the dimensions and mode of acquiring the share of social wealth of which they dispose. Classes are groups of people one of which can appropriate the labor of another owing to the different places they occupy in a definite system of social economy.

After 1956, however, class has taken on a new meaning in socialist China. First of all, ***class was individualized*** and divorced from the structural location. Class became a label that every Chinese carried on his or her back in socialist China. One's class designation is formally stored in a class dossier, an official record kept by the party-state on every Chinese citizen. This class designation has enormous implications for one's life chances, as a whole set of class-discriminatory institutions and practices aiming at hampering the life-chances of those social aliens (like the landlord class) were systematically put in pace in all aspects important for everyday life — education, housing employment, food rations, political participation, social activities (like marriage and friendship) and political activities (like whether one will become a target of attack in political campaigns).

Although theoretically speaking class labels were not supposed to be inherited beyond two generations, "class origin" as defined by family connection or bloodline was in actuality inherited patrilineally. As Yiching Wu (2007) remarks, "class analysis, once a powerful instrument of revolutionary practice, produced ossified classification schemes and specimens which, essentially frozen in time, bore little if any relationship with actual class contradiction".

Second, ***class was politicized and "behaviorized"***. Following the socialization of private property in socialist China after 1956, the source of class tensions was said to be located mostly in the super-structure and that "politics" must be in command. This implied a primary focus within the superstructure on the politics of ideology (with class defined in terms of political behavior), and to value class standpoint and class behavior more than economic position.

Beginning in the late 1950s, Mao has started to emphasize the *behavioral dimension of class* (like whether one practice unity with workers and peasants, or whether one is modest, prudent, and guard against arrogance and impetuosity) as he tried to make a new class analysis, consistently holding back from a full-fledged examination of the structural roots of class in the party-state.

During the Cultural Revolution in the late 1960s, Mao chose to emphasize political behavior as the measure of class, saying that political behavior was even more important than economic position in identifying class. This is because Mao believed that a person can transcend a special economic environment to serve a different class, thus renegade workers could assist the bourgeoisie, turn into class enemies and members of the new class. This emphasis upon behavioral outcomes permitted Mao's anti-bureaucratic attack to be justified in terms of the "force of habit" or "cultural contamination" left over from the old society, rather than demanding a costly effort to dismantle the entire state apparatus.

Third, ***class becomes an overloaded tool*** which can explain everything. In post-1956 China, all social conflicts were discussed as if they were aspects of class struggle. Thus, gender struggle, ethnic struggle, national struggle, cultural struggle, and spatial struggle were all aspects of class struggle. For the radical leftists, they believe that they must wage continuous warfare against the class enemy in order to protect Chinese socialism, but the battle is made more difficult because the adversary is often a "hidden class enemy". There are instances where the class enemies come out personally to fight the battle. But more frequently, they perpetrate sabotage by making use of their influence in the ideological sphere. For the radical leftists, the protracted and all-pervasive conflict among social classes can be won for the revolution only when the Chinese constantly ring the imaginary bell of class struggle in our minds.

Not only class struggle exists everywhere, *class struggle will never end.* In criticizing the so-called "theory of the dying out of class struggle" of Liu Shaoqi, radical leftists during the Cultural Revolution insisted that class struggle will persist for a very long time. The radical leftists argued that class struggle does not end with the establishment of socialism and the concomitant weakening of distinctions among the relations of citizens to the means of production. In part, this is because the impact of private property is felt long after its formal abolition: "Although the seal of the landlord and the bourgeoisie has been snatched away from them, and the means of production are not in their hands, these persons still live, and their hearts are not dead" (*Renmin Ribao*, 1968, p. 4).

In sum, the new class analysis in post-1956 China, especially during the 1966–1975 Cultural Revolution, has made the concept of class more individualized, politicized, and behaviorized, and the concept of class became an overloaded tool which can explain any social conflict, class conflict exists everywhere and continues forever. What are the problems of this new class analysis in post-1956 China?

PROBLEMS OF THE NEW CLASS ANALYSIS

The problem of Mao's new class theory arose from the elusiveness of its central concept: political behavior. A political conception of class was that its class behavior could only be loosely defined, thus encouraging the casual use of class analysis to stigmatize against any political rival. Yiching Wu (2007) also observed that the Cultural Revolution and its prevailing discourse of class lacked a very clear focus as defined in structural terms. Its politics of class was too broad, and the political targets during the Cultural Revolution were often too diffuse.

For example, two most important concerns for judging the quality of political behavior in identifying a proletariat are: "whether the person followed the socialist road and party leadership". This formulation, of course, begs the question of class criteria, as it is not necessarily evident what exactly constitutes supports for the socialist road or party leadership. If such criteria ever exist, they are easily mutable, highly subjective, and subject to abuse during the Cultural Revolution.

As Kraus (1981, p. 109) points out, distinguishing proletarian from bourgeois behavior was difficult, even when sincerely attempted. When applied hastily in the course of political struggle during the Cultural Revolution, the behavioral emphasis was often a source of mischief, as good socialist action may be variously defined. The repeated emphasis upon class struggle often encouraged the rhetorical escalation of routine social conflict into life-and-death struggles between proletarians and bourgeoisie. When the official language of class conflict was superimposed upon local disagreements, there was often considerable uncertainty about how to use its class categories, a phenomenon which tended to strengthen existing factional tendencies among Mao's youthful rebels (Montaperto, 1972, pp. 592–593).

The new class analysis was too easily used to turn weakened political adversaries into scapegoats, badgering old enemies in the name of socialist revolution. In the absence of unambiguous guidelines for class identification, many cadres succumbed to the temptation to assign labels on the basis of personal animosities or ambitions. In this respect, extremely politicized class analysis encouraged much political persecution of individuals in the late 1960s.

On the other hand, the mass movement during the most iconoclastic days of the Cultural Revolution mobilized in the names of "class struggle" attacked against everything and anyone. Pushed to its radical extreme, the concept of "class" melted down under its own unbearable weight of being licensed to target and attack everything, eventually and inevitably shattering the "class" concept itself (Wu, 2007).

The different waves of class struggles during the Cultural Revolution had deeply divided the Chinese society and resulted in numerous factional struggles and random violence. Needless to stress, these waves of class struggle had also deeply delegitimized the communist party-state.

In sum, after nationalization and collectivization in post-1956 China, the party-state monopolized the economic, political, and social resources in the society. The Chinese people were completely dependent on the state not only for job and income but also for services, status, and influence in the community. The formation of a statist society exerted a profound impact of state–society relations. When property-based classes and other political organizations were either eliminated or absorbed in the state structure, there was no intermediation between the state and society. The party-state could directly control society and impose its policies on the society. Thus, the common feature of this statist society are the politicization of social/economic issues as class issues, the constant mobilization of individuals, and rupture conflict (the sudden rise of fall of highly intensive and violent conflict in political campaigns). It is, therefore, interesting to note that even when the objective property-based antagonistic classes were eroded by 1956, the subjective categories of "class" and "class struggle" were used all the time by the radical red guards during the Cultural Revolution during the period 1966–1976.

In the late 1970s, there was the passing away of the first generation of peasant revolutionaries. In the 1950s and the 1960s, these peasant revolutionaries had pushed for radical egalitarian experiment to socialist policies. In the late 1970s, they were replaced by a whole new generation of career-minded bureaucrats who saw no necessity to be an enemy of the capitalist core states; they generally accepted the capitalist order and gave up the revolutionary aspirations of the Maoists. This new generation of bureaucrats has been labeled "economic reformers" by the core states.

However, since the radical Maoists focused on class struggles and political campaigns, they had neglected to promote economic development. When economic output and productivity in the 1970s could no longer be increased through political mobilization, and when incessant class struggles had not only deeply divided the Chinese society but also led to the de-legitimation of the party-state, there was a call for a "Four Modernization" program to jump start the Chinese economy.

Subsequently, when the old generation of peasant revolutionaries passed away, and when the United States lowered its hostility, economic reformers adopted a set of neo-liberalism policies to open its door for foreign investment, thus started a whole new re-entry phase into the capitalist world-economy. The next chapter will discuss how the re-integration into the capitalist world-economy has exerted a profound impact on China's social classes and class conflict in the post-1978 era. Many social classes (such as the capitalists and the new middle class), which were destroyed in the withdrawal phase, have managed a dramatic come back in the reintegration phase. On the other hand, the winners (such as the workers and peasants) in the withdrawal phase have become losers in the reintegration phase (see Table 3.1 on page 38).

Chapter 3

CLASS AND CLASS CONFLICT IN POST-SOCIALIST CHINA SINCE 1978*

Like other countries in the developing world in the late 1970s, China has faithfully carried out the policies of neoliberalism when it re-entered the capitalist world-economy in the late 1970s. The Chinese party-state set up institutional frameworks to guarantee private property rights and promoted free markets and free trades, with the hope that the Chinese economy could be invigorated and compete successfully in the world market.

However, unlike other countries in the developing world, China did not lose out during the so-called lost decades of neoliberalism in the 1980s and 1990s. Instead, China has undergone rapid and sustained economic development in the last three decades of the 20th century. China's development has been remarkable for a number of reasons. In the first place, its gross domestic product has increased at close to 10% per year since 1978, and the country managed to reduce the share of population living on less than US$1 per day from 64% in 1981 to 16% by 2006, or effectively lifting 400 million people out of absolute poverty (UNDP, 2006). The rapid growth rate was matched nowhere in the world except by the so-called Asian miracle economies of Korea, Taiwan, Singapore, and Hong Kong.

In the second place, although the Chinese economy has its share of problems, such as the re-emergence of social classes and class

---

* This chapter is an updated version of an earlier paper co-authored by Alvin Y. So and Cindy Chu (So and Chu, 2012). I want to thank Cindy Chu for her permission to include the co-authored paper in this volume.

conflict, it succeeded in upgrading its technological capability and escaped the threat of foreign domination. Over the years, not only has China become the global factory for inexpensive consumer goods, it has also enticed BP, General Motors, Intel, Microsoft, Oracle, and other corporations to locate part of their research and development facilities in China. Furthermore, despite the importance of foreign investors both as producers aiming at the global market, or as retailers targeting at the domestic one, foreign capital remains largely a junior partner in China's development project.

In the third place, despite the downfall of the former Soviet Union and Eastern Europe, China's communist party-state has continued to provide leadership to the country; China has avoided the regime change and political chaos that had happened to its socialist cousins in Eastern Europe.

As a result, by the first decade of the 21st century researchers began to characterize China as a "rising, new economic superpower" and reported that "China surged past the United States to become the world's largest automobile market" (Holz, 2006; Wines, 2010b). The world press began to speak of the G-2 (the United States and China) who in effect share world power (Wallerstein, 2010). Some researchers even welcome China's regional and global emergence as it could serve as a counter-weight to the U.S.-driven neoliberal and militarized capitalism (Silver and Arrighi, 2000).

This chapter will pose the following research question: What is the impact of the re-integration in the capitalist world-economy on China's social classes and class conflict? In what ways do China's patterns of state–class relationship help her to avoid the pitfalls of neoliberalism to become one of the economic powerhouses of the 21st century? This chapter's argument is that China has pursued a different mode of neoliberalism — a different form of configuration of class–state relationship that can be called **state neoliberalism** — from the mainstream neoliberalism that is promoted in the Washington Consensus model. In the following sections, it will first delineate the distinctive features of state neoliberalism. Then, it will examine how the neoliberalism project historically emerged in China in the 1980s and deepened in the 1990s, and then how this further transformed to state neoliberalism at the turn of the 21st century.

To begin with, let us explain our conception of state neoliberalism and how it is different from the neoliberalism project in Washington Consensus.

NEOLIBERALISM AND STATE NEOLIBERALISM

Before the late 1970s, capitalism in the North took the form what David Harvey (2005) called "*embedded liberalism*". In order to solve the acute economic and social problems created by the unfettered market during the 1930s depression, the advanced capitalist state had to take a more active role in managing the economy to provide full employment as well as to avoid wide upswings and downswings of the market. In embedded liberalism, the state is taking on more and more roles (like providing more welfare and social services, strengthening workers' trade unions, imposing more regulations on the market, and imposing higher taxes on the capitalist class). Thus, capital was induced to compromise and have a new social contract with the working class, with the result the capital was embedded in a web of social and political constraints in a new regulatory regime that served to control its "greedy" profit-making behavior. After World War II, a variety of liberal, social democratic, and dirigiste welfare states emerged in Western Europe and the United States that exemplify this embedded liberalism trend.

According to Harvey (2005), *neoliberalism* is a new **class project** through which the capitalist class fights back against the high taxes and the strict regulations of the state as well as the "rigidities" imposed by the state and the trade union on production relations. On the one hand, neoliberalism is aimed to liberalize the market so members of the capitalist class could have more freedom to hire and fire their workers, more freedom to expand their trading and investment within the state boundary or beyond in the global space. In the late 1970s, neoliberalism was accompanied by deregulation, privatization, and the marketization of social services. On the other hand, neoliberalism is aimed to downsize the state where the role of the state is confined to set up and preserve the institution for market liberalism. Thus, Harvey (2005, p. 7) uses the term "neoliberal state" to refer to "a state apparatus whose fundamental mission was to facilitate condition for profitable capital accumulation on the part of both domestic and foreign capital".

In the North, neoliberalism emerged in advanced capitalist societies where both the state and the capitalist class were fully institutionalized and were the two most powerful players in their societies. Neoliberalism was a new project prompted by members of the capitalist class who wanted to revamp the unfettered market when confronted by a crisis of capital accumulation in the 1970s. As "neoliberalism" replaces "embedded liberalism", state–market relation shift from a situation of state domination to one of market domination.

The historical context through which neoliberalism emerged in China, however, was totally different to that in the North. China is a state socialist country where property was pre-dominantly owned by the state and the Collective. In addition, as explained in the previous chapter, China in the early 1970s had just gone through a devastating Cultural Revolution, the primary aim of which was to suppress the capitalist market and destroy the capitalist class. Thus, the private sector was almost non-existent and the capitalist class was very weak at the onset of the reform. The market institution, therefore, had to be constructed from almost nothing. Given this scenario, which agent had the capacity to re-create the market institution in 1970s China in the aftermath of the Cultural Revolution, where anti-capitalist sentiment was still very strong?

Whereas the capitalist class has been the dominant agency for neoliberalism in the North, the communist party-state had to take the driving seat to propel neoliberalism forward in China. During the initial stage of the reform in the 1980s, the communist party-state did carry out neoliberalism policy wholeheartedly. However, when the Chinese society responded to neoliberal policies with waves of social resistance and class conflict at the turn of 21st century, the communist party-state had a second thought and adopted state neoliberalism in order to attain a more harmonious society.

Thus, I coined the term *state neoliberalism* to highlight the contrast between China's experience of neoliberalism, and that of the North. Obviously, state neoliberalism is a highly contradictory term: Since the party-state still claims to be communist and stands on the side of the worker class and the peasantry, it could not have possibly carried out all sorts of neoliberal policies to assault workers and peasants to undermine their basis of class support. When the negative impacts of neoliberalism led to waves of class conflict among urban workers and countryside peasants and threatened the survival of the party-state, the party-state had to institute state neoliberalism — like more taxes and more regulations, more redistribution of resources to the countryside — to restrain the excess of neoliberalism. As such, it will be interesting to study how the class contradiction of neoliberalism in a post-socialist state has led to an oscillation between market-led and state-led developments in China, and how the party-state has handled this class contradiction over the past three decades, leading not only to the surprising continuation of the Chinese communist party-state, but also to the rise of China as a contending power in the capitalist world-economy.

NEOLIBERALISM CAPITALISM IN CHINA IN THE LATE 1970s AND THE 1980s

Like other countries in the North, South, and East, the impulse to carry out neoliberalism policy was irresistible when the state faced the crisis of capital accumulation in the 1970s and the 1980s. Thus, the Chinese communist party-state started the reforms to reinvent and liberate the market from the state as well as to re-integrate China into the capitalist world-economy in order to speed up capital accumulation. It was with the above neoliberal mindset that the Chinese state leaders carried out the following policies during the neoliberal era in the late 1970s and the 1980s:

- **Decollectivization**. In the countryside, agricultural communes were dismantled in favor of an individualized "personal responsibility system". Peasant families were given plots of land to cultivate, and they were responsible for their own gains and losses. They were also encouraged to sell their products to rural markets, engage in rural industries, and seek work in nearby township enterprises. Decollectivization has created a *rich peasant class* that capitalized on the abundant supply of surplus laborers in the countryside.

- **Township and village enterprises** were created out of the former commune assets, and these became centers of entrepreneurialism, flexible labor practices, and open market competition. The expansion of the private sector has given rise to a middle class (*petty-bourgeoisie getihu* employing less than 10 workers and to a *capitalist class* (entrepreneurs employing 10 workers or more).

- **Proletarianization of peasants**. At the same time, the loss of collective social rights in the countryside meant that the peasants had to face burdensome user charges for schools, medical care, and the like. Forced to seek work elsewhere after the end of collectivism, rural migrants flooded — illegally and without the right of residency — into the cities to form an immense labor reserve (a "floating population" of indeterminate legal status). China is now in the midst of the largest mass migration the world has ever seen (Chan, 2003). Facilitated by the loosening of the household registration, this rural "floating population" is vulnerable to super-exploitation and puts downward pressure on the wages of urban workers (Pun, 1999).

- **Marketization** policy to restore/expand the market. A new labor market was introduced to the Chinese economy in the late 1980s, creating a flexible labor force that would be responsive to the ups and downs of the market. After the labor market was set up, the state enterprises also underwent reforms so they were no longer required to provide life-long employment and job security to their workers; they were given the autonomy to hire and fire workers in the name of enhancing productivity and efficiency as called upon by neoliberalism. The creation of the labor market meant that *the working class* would need to sell its labor market for a labor.

- **Fiscal Decentralization and the weakening of the central state**. In the mid-1980s, provincial, municipality, county and township governments were subject to a bottom-up revenue-sharing system that required localities to submit only a portion of the revenues to the upper level, and then they were allowed to retain all, or at the least, most of the reminder. This fiscal decentralization policy made local states become independent fiscal entities that had the unprecedented right to use the revenue they retained. As a result, fiscal decentralization had considerably weakened the central state's extractive capacity. The Chinese state was unable to control the extra-budgetary funds of the local governments, and its relative share of tax revenues had decreased to the extent that the Central state had lost effective control over China's economic life (Wang and Hu, 2001; Oi, 1992).

- **Opening up and spatial differentiation**. There was an open-door policy toward foreign investments. It began with the establishment of four special economic zones (SEZs) in 1979, the opening of 14 coastal cities and Hainan Island in 1984, and the extension to three delta areas (Pearl River Delta, Yangtze River Delta, and Yellow River Delta) in 1985. The open-door policy has laid the economic foundation for the recreation of *a foreign capitalist class* engaging either in sole ownership or in joint venture with Chinese enterprises. The combination of decentralization and opening up has led to a very uneven pattern of spatial development in China, with rapid economic growth taking place mostly along the eastern coastal subregions. These subregions were characterized by an *extrovert* economy, i.e., their economies were driven by foreign direct investment and export-led industrialization, and their economic growth relied upon their integration with the global commodity chains (Chen, 2005).

- **Expansion of the new middle class.** The above process of decentralization, enterprise reforms, and the success of township enterprises has greatly expanded the size of *the new middle class* (corporate professionals such as mid-level managers and accountants). The expansion of higher education institutions and the service sector in turn has greatly expanded the size of another segment of the new middle class (service professionals such as teachers, social workers, and journalists).

In sum, in post-socialist China since 1978, the neoliberal reform policies adopted during the re-entry phase have re-created the social classes that the socialist party-state took pain to destroy or weaken during the withdrawal phase (see Table 3.1).

Through the above processes of decollectivization and proletarianization, marketization, fiscal decentralization, opening up and spatial differentiation, post-socialist China was clearly moving toward the neoliberal capitalist model. On the one hand, the state was being downsized and its capacity was being weakened. On the other hand, the private sector and the various (labor, capital, and finance) markets were expanding rapidly and the Chinese economy reintegrated with the capitalist world-economy.

Table 3.1:   China's social classes and the capitalist world-economy.

Withdrawal phase	Policy	Target class (to eliminate/weaken)
	Core hostilities	Foreign capitalists
	Land reforms	Landlord
	Collectivization	Rich peasants
	Nationalization	Bourgeois
	Hundred Flowers Campaign	New Middle Class

Reintegration phase	Policy	Target class (to create/strengthen)
	Open-door policies — Special economic zones, joint ventures	Foreign capitalist
	Decollectivization, Self-responsibility system	Rich peasant
	Urban reforms — Reintroduction of the market, State enterprise reform	Cadre–capitalist
	Expansion of the higher Education system	New middle class

Like other neoliberal states, China suffered considerable cost during her initial march toward neoliberal capitalism in the 1980s. A decade of market "reforms" already led to many serious economic problems, such as inflation, unemployment, corruption, and tax invasion. Inflation was over 30% in 1988 and 1989 when the state tried to decontrol commodity prices. Unemployment became a problem when the bankrupted enterprises discharged workers. Workers showed signs of discontent as reforms began to exert tighter control over work schedule and raised work quotas. A government source estimated that 70% of enterprises became rich through profiteering and speculation, while another source revealed that the private sector had evaded from 70% to 80% of their taxes (So and Hua, 1992).

In the late 1980s, the above economic problems and social grievances had triggered a democracy movement that led to a confrontation between the protesters and the party-state in the Tiananmen Square. The Tiananmen incident was a first major challenge to the Chinese communist party-state during the Post-Mao era. It led to bloody suppression of the protesters and serious political division within the party-state between the so-called reformist faction (which is pro-neoliberal reform) and the conservative faction (which is skeptical to such reform). What then happened after the Tiananmen incident?

RE-BUILDING THE STATE AND THE DEEPENING OF NEOLIBERAL CAPITALISM IN THE 1990s

In contrast to the image of a weakened state in the neoliberal literature, the Chinese state has considerably strengthened its managerial and fiscal capacity during the aftermath of the Tiananmen Incident. A new "cadre responsibility system" was instituted in the early 1990s by the central party-state to strengthen its control over the evaluation and monitoring of local leaders. County party secretaries and township heads sign performance contracts, pledge to attain certain targets laid down by higher levels, and are held personally responsible for attaining those targets. There are different contracts for different fields, such as industrial development, agricultural development, tax collection, family planning, and social order. The Chinese party-state has the capacity to be selective, i.e., to implement its priority policies, to control the appointment of its key local leaders, and to target strategically important areas. Thus, Maria Edin (2003, p. 36) argues that "state capacity, defined here as the capacity to control and monitor lower-level agents, has increased in China, and that the Chinese communist party (CCP) is capable of greater institutional adaptability that it is usually given credit for".

In addition, the state has strengthened its fiscal capacity. The central party-state introduced a "Tax Sharing Scheme" (TSS) in 1994 to redress the center–local imbalance in fiscal matters (Yep, 2007). The TSS is aimed at improving the center's control over the economy by increasing "two ratios" — the share of budgetary revenue in the GDP and the central share in total budgetary revenue. It seems that the TSS did succeed in raising the "two ratios" (Loo and Chow, 2006), thus helping to arrest the decline of fiscal foundation of the center and increase the extractive capacity of the central party-state. Zheng (2004, pp. 118–119) argues that the TSS has shifted fiscal power from the provinces to the center, so "now, it is the provinces that rely on the central government for revenue".

In addition, in contrast to the neoliberal doctrine's calling for less intervention, the Chinese state has intervened more into the economy. It has engaged in debt-financed investments in huge mega-projects to transform physical infrastructures. Astonishing rates of urbanization (no fewer than 42 cities have expanded beyond the 1 million population mark since 1992) have required huge investments of fixed capital. New subway systems and highways are being built in major cities, and 8,500 miles of new railroad are proposed to link the interior to the economically dynamic coastal zone. China is also trying to build an interstate highway system more extensive than America in just 15 years, while practically every large city is building or has just completed a big new airport. These mega-projects have the potential to absorb surpluses of capital and labor for several years to come (Harvey, 2005, p. 132). It is these massive debt-financing infrastructural and fixed-capital formation projects that make the Chinese state depart from the neoliberal orthodoxy and act like a Keynesian state.

Furthermore, after the party-state has strengthened its capacity and played a more active role in upgrading the economy, it also pushed for a deepening of neoliberalism capitalism. In the first wave of neoliberal reforms in the 1980s, the reform policies were aimed mostly to expand the private sector; they had left the public sector largely intact. Thus, the reformers in the 1980s used the term "market socialism" to stress that China was still socialist because it had a dominant public sector and the party-state was still in control of the strategic sector (or the commanding height) of the Chinese economy.

However, the party-state turned to the public sector and pushed forward the following policies in the late 1990s:

- *Privatization and corporatization* policy to cut the size of the state sector and to increase the size of the private sector. In the 1990s, the state-owned enterprises (SOEs) were undergoing corporatization, so they were no longer dependent on the state for funding and had to operate independently in the market. After corporatization, the SOEs were asked to run like an independent private profit-making enterprise; they could go bankrupt if they were losing money (So, 2005). The SOEs were given the green light to lay-off workers, to increase the intensity of work and productivity, and to cut worker's benefits if they found it necessary to remain competitive in the market. The late 1990s observed the layoff of millions of state workers and the cutting back of their benefits.
- *Commodification of human services.* Whereas the Maoist state provided human services (like housing, health care, welfare, education, pension, etc.) on need-based and free of charge to all citizens, the post-reform state treated human services as a commodity to be distributed to people on market principles.

Housing, for example, is no longer provided to the state workers for free. Instead, workers are now asked to find their own housing in the newly emerged private housing markets. Likewise, workers are now asked to pay a part of the costs for services in most welfare fields and social insurance, such as pension, medical care and the newly created unemployment insurance, higher education, and many personal services (Guan, 2000).

- *Deepening of liberalization.* Petras (2006) points out that China joining the World Trade Organization (WTO) is likely to lead to a further dismantling of the state sector, dismantling of trade barriers and removal of subsidies, savaging of the countryside, near unquestioning orientation toward the export market strategy, and consolidation of foreign production as the leading force in the Chinese economy (see also Hart-Landsberg and Burkett, 2004).

The deepening of neoliberal capitalism in China has further intensified class conflict in Chinese society. A class-divided society quickly emerged in post-socialist China. First, there is a rapid class differentiation in both the countryside and the city. In the countryside, a relatively homogeneous peasant stratum in the Maoist era is now split into a rich peasant class and a poor peasant class. No longer able to earn a living on their tiny family farms, many poor peasants have to work for rich peasants as laborers in their farms or as workers in their village enterprises. In the cities, a relatively homogeneous urbanite is now split into a capitalist class, an old middle class of self-employed and small employer, and a working class subdivided into permanent urban workers and temporary migrant workers. In the private and collective enterprises, temporary migrants work in a capitalist situation not too much different from their counterparts in the early stages of the Industrial Revolution. They have to work very long hours, get only minimum wages, obey strict work disciplines, secure work on a day-to-day basis, and are unable to form labor unions to protect their interests. Studies have shown that the capitalist class frequently invokes the factors of gender (like paying female workers less than male workers), ethnicity (like hiring out-of-province migrant workers than local workers), and kinship ties (like recruit workers from the same village as that of the foreman) in order to facilitate its control over the workers (Pun, 2001).

Second, aside from class differentiation, there is a growing trend of class polarization. Many studies show that the rich are getting richer and the poor are getting poorer. At the top, there are millionaires and even billionaires. At the bottom, there is an underclass of temporary migrants in the city and poverty is widespread in inland provinces. In the early 1980s, China was among the world's most egalitarian societies. By the mid-1990s, the inequalities of income distribution in China had not only already exceeded the inequality found in the transition economies in Eastern Europe and the high-income countries of Western Europe and North America, but also in China's Asian neighbors such as India, Pakistan, and Indonesia (Wang and Hu, 1999).

ANOTHER WAVE OF SOCIAL RESISTANCES TO THE DEEPENING OF NEOLIBERAL CAPITALISM IN THE 1990s

Starting in the 1990s, conflict has begun to take the rudimentary form of class conflict, organizing along class line, and raising class issues. In the countryside, there are many rural protests from poor peasants complaining about high taxes, irregular taxes, low prices of their agricultural products, encroachment of their land and house, the state's IOUs, etc. In the city, there are many protests from workers complaining about their layoffs, the closing down of their enterprises, the reduction of their wages and benefits, the abuses by their managers, etc. In 1989, workers joined hands with the middle class students, intellectuals, and capitalists to wage a robust democracy movement complaining corruption, high rates of inflation, and the lack of independent unions (Lee, 2000; Perry and Selden, 2000). In May 2001, a report issued by a Central Committee research group spoke of "tense" relations between the party and the people. The report spoke about the collapse of state-owned industry, a social safety net incapable of dealing with millions of unemployed, strained relations with China's ethnic minorities, a restive peasantry and an unjust legal system (Pomfret, 2001).

When neoliberal reforms were deepened during the late 1990s, workers, peasants, and the middle class were getting restless, their criticisms of the problems of neoliberalism were more upfront and blunt, and their protests and demonstrations were getting more widespread and violent. These societal resistances got reflected in the party-state. In June 1998, 35 members of the elite standing Committee of the National People's Congress (NPC) presented an emergency resolution to the top leaders of the CCP, accusing the government and party of violating workers' "right of existence" and "trampling the worker peasant alliance", and alluding to widespread protest and opposition to China's program of economic liberalization (Liew, 2001; Nonini, 2008).

Despite the above processes of class differentiation, class polarization, and class conflict, however, the class-divided society that re-emerged since 1978 was different from its predecessor during the first half of the 20th century. Pre-1949 China was a class-divided society embedded in a weak state. Thus, social classes and class conflict had a much larger role to play in the promoting of political change and societal transformation. Post-1978 China, however, is a class-divided society embedded in a strong Leninist party-state, thus social classes and class conflict are mediated through the state and shaped by the state.

The above challenges to the party-state happened at the right time because the party was undergoing an elite transition. In 2002, President Jiang Zemin's leadership team was replaced by Hu Jintao and Wen Jiabao. According to Joseph Cheng (2007), Hu and Wen's ideal was to return to the good old days of the 1950s when the Maoist Party was in full control, and the vast majority of party cadres were uncorrupt, dedicated and selfless.

By the early 2000s, Hu and Wen began to institute a new mode of neoliberal policies — what can be called *state neoliberalism* — in response to the escalation of social resistances and class conflict in Chinese society.

THE TRANSITION FROM NEOLIBERALISM TO STATE NEOLIBERALISM AT THE TURN OF THE 21ST CENTURY

In contrast to the neoliberal doctrine which calls for the dismantling of the welfare state, the Chinese party-state under the leadership of Hu and Wen presented a new policy of "building a new socialist countryside" and a "harmonious society" in 2006 (Saich, 2007). The above policy is significant because it could signal a change of ideological orientation of the Chinese state (Kahn, 2006). Whereas the pre-2006 Chinese party-state adopted a neoliberal orientation, it is now moving toward a more balanced one between economic growth and social development. While market reforms would continue, this new policy indicates that the state would play a more active role in moderating the negative impacts of marketization. In the new policy, the state will need to include "the people and environment" in its developmental plan, and not just focus narrowly on GNP indicators and economic growth.

Thus, the new policy advocates a transfer of resources from the state to strengthen the fiscal foundation of the countryside. Not only was the agricultural tax abolished to help relieve the burden on farmers, but the state increased its rural expenditure by 15% (to US$15 billion) to bankroll guaranteed minimum living allowances for farmers, and an 87% hike (to US$4 billion) for the health-care budget (Liu and Ansfield, 2007). These policies indicate a massive infusion of funding from the state onto the peasants and rural areas. In addition, there is a de-commodification of human services. Rural residents would no longer have to pay many miscellaneous charges levied by schools; fees at primary schools will be abolished as part of a nationwide campaign to eliminate them in the countryside for the first nine years of education. The state would also increase the subsidies for rural health cooperatives that will be available in 80% of the rural counties by 2008. For now, rural residents have to pay market rates at the villages' private clinics and most of them do not even have medical insurance and spend more than 80% of their cash on health care (Liu and Ansfield, 2007). Furthermore, the new policy is aimed at reducing social inequality, especially the widening gap between the countryside and the city. Thus, pensions are to be made available for everyone, not just those enjoying a privileged status as registered by urban residents. Over the past two years, the state has also been promoting the spread of Minimum Living Standard Assistance for the rural population. This is potentially a highly significant development, opening up for the first time the real possibility of instituting a social safety net that covers the whole of the population, whether urban or rural (*The Economists*, 2006; Hussain, 2005).

Unlike the neoliberal state in other parts of the world, China has a strong state machinery. Although a cadre–capitalist class has emerged at the local level when state managers are asked to promote local development, so-called "local state corporatism" by Oi (1992), this cadre–capitalist class has failed to capture the central party-state. Thus, the central party-state can still uphold the moral high ground of state socialism, going after the capitalist for tax evasion and the breaking of environmental laws, standing on the side of the workers by strengthening the labor laws, and standing on the side of peasants by cutting rural taxes and relocating more resources to the countryside. The party-state at the center blames corrupt officials for causing social unrests at the local level. The central Chinese state is also highly autonomous in the sense that it is not "captured" by vested economic interests at the local level. The old generation of capitalists was largely destroyed in the Communist Revolution and later in the Cultural Revolution. The nascent capitalist class that has just emerged in the market reforms of the 1980s and 1990s is still too weak and too dependent on the state to pose any challenge. In addition, the Chinese state has the capacity to carry out its developmental plans. Since it owns the banks and controls the financial sector, it has powerful policy tools at its disposal which makes the cooperation of indigenous business more likely: access to cheap credit, protection from external competition, and assisted access to export markets are all levers that the Chinese state can use to ensure business compliance with the governmental goals. Since the Chinese corporations have a high debt/equity ratio, even the threat of withdrawal of state loans would be serious.

Second, different from the neoliberal state in Washington Consensus, the Chinese state has actively intervened in the economy.

The state has become the engine for powering capital accumulation. Aside from debt finance and infrastructure construction, the Chinese central state also develops plans for strategic development, decrees prices and regulates the movement of capital, and shares risks and underwrites research and development.

Third, unlike other neoliberal state, the Chinese state has actively mobilized the ideology of nationalism and defines itself as carrying out a national project to make China strong and powerful. In the post-reform era, China was experiencing an ideological vacuum since the state could no longer be legitimized by Marxism or communism. Thus, nationalism became the state's only hope to get the support of the Chinese masses. The Chinese state seems to believe that the best response is to build a strong sense of national cohesiveness based on cultural heritage and tradition rather than to develop a nationalism based solely on hostility toward the outside world. Nationalism, however, can cut both ways. The Chinese state knows well that excessive nationalism might not only undercut the communist party's ability to rule but also disrupt China's paramount foreign policy objective of creating a long-term peaceful environment for its modernization program. The Chinese state's concern is reflected in its rejection of a more radical nationalism, such as that advocated by the authors of *The China that Can Say No,* as well as in its efforts to control anti-Japanese sentiment. Indeed, China's response to the Japanese provocation over the visit of the shrine was far more restrained than in Taiwan and Hong Kong. The Chinese state's concern that nationalism had to be controlled was also evident in its efforts to restrain anti-Americanism in the aftermath of the NATO bombing of the Chinese embassy in Yugoslavia (Ogden, 2003).

Fourth, unlike the embedded social democratic states in the North that see themselves as a protector of citizenship rights, the Chinese state adopts authoritarian policies to discipline labor, suppress labor protests, and deactivate civil society in order to maintain a favorable environment for attracting foreign investment and facilitating capital accumulation. It seems authoritarianism is unavoidable in export-led industrialization because labor subordination is an important means to cheapen labor and make the working class docile. Otherwise, the exports of the East Asian developmental states would not be competitive in the world economy, and transnational corporations would not relocate their labor-intensive production to East Asia. It is ironic that the Chinese neoliberal state, with its tightly organized Leninist party-state machinery, has proven to be very effective in co-opting labor activists, dividing the working class, and silencing the labor protests.

In short, China's experience of neoliberalism is unique: It is different from both the neoliberal state in the Washington Consensus and the embedded liberal state in the North. The Chinese state neoliberalism has a strong state machinery with a high degree of state autonomy and a strong capacity to carry out its goals. It greatly intervenes in the economy through developmental planning, deficit investment, export promotion, and strategic industrialization. It is also highly nationalistic and authoritarian, suppressing labor protests and limiting popular struggles.

CONCLUSION

David Harvey (2005, p. 1) points out that the period 1978–1980 was a turning point in China's social and economic history. In 1978, Deng Xiaoping, the leader of the CCP took the first momentous step towards the liberalization of a communist-ruled economy. The path that Deng defined was to transform China in two decades from a closed backwater to an open center of neoliberal capitalism in the global economy. The first decade of neoliberal reforms, however, had led to serious economic and social problems in the Chinese society, triggered off robust democracy protests at the Tiananmen Square in 1989 to challenge the rule of the CCP.

In the aftermath of the 1989 Tiananmen incident, the party-state tried hard to re-strengthen itself. It instituted a "cadre responsibility system" to improve local governance and a "tax sharing scheme" to readdress the center–local imbalance in fiscal matters. After political order and economic growth were restored, the party-state was determined to push for a deepening of neoliberal capitalism (such as privatization and corporation, commodification of social services, and the entry into WTO) in the mid 1990s.

By the late 1990s, however, China began to feel the pains of a neoliberal economy. First, there was super-exploitation of labor power, particularly of young women migrants from rural areas. Wage levels in China were extremely low, and conditions of labor were not sufficiently regulated, and were despotic and exploitative. Moreover, China became one of the world's most unequal societies. Neoliberal market reforms had rapidly led to disparities in income among different classes, social strata, and regions, thus leading rapidly to social polarization. Formal measures of social inequalities, such as Gini Coefficient, confirm that China had traveled the path from one of the most equalitarian societies to chronic inequality, all in the span of 20 years (Harvey, 2005, p. 143). In the late 1990s, the above contradictions led to many different kinds of class conflicts in society, as shown by the increasing call to regulate the market and by the growing numbers of labor protests, peasant demonstrations, social movements, and other large-scale social disturbances.

In the light of the above contradictions and discontents, the Chinese Communist party-state had a second thought about its neoliberal policies since the 1990s. Besides, neoliberalism was increasingly coming under attack and losing its creditability in the global economy. In the East, the "shock therapy" — which called for the dismantling of the centrally planned economy as soon as possible — not only did not work but also led to the downfall of the communist states in Eastern Europe. In the West, the anti-globalization movement was greatly empowered by its success in Seattle. In China, the Chinese party-state in the late 1990s began to reverse its neoliberal policies and started to build up a developmental state. After the party-state strengthened its fiscal capacity, it engaged in debt-financing investments in huge mega-projects to transform infrastructures and declared a new policy of "building a new socialist countryside" to address the issues of poverty and inequality in the rural areas.

Besides, the situation in China was not desperate. The Chinese state was not under any threat of foreign invasion, did not incur any large amount of foreign debt, and faced no immediate threat of acing any rebellion from below. As such, the Chinese state still had the autonomy and capacity to propose and implement various developmental policies "from above". For instance, the state could selectively introduce different types of developmental policies, could vary the speed of the market reforms, could expand or limit the space of opening up to transnational capital, and, most importantly, could still have the freedom of adjusting (or even reversing) its policies if they were not working.

The asymmetrical power relationship between the state and the other classes has also given the state a free hand to try different developmental policies over the past few decades. The capitalist class is too small, too weak, and too dependent on the state to be the agent of historical transformation in China. The capitalist class is politically impotent to capture the state to carry out the neoliberal path of development. Facing growing labor unrest and popular struggle against such abuses as child labor in the coal mines, discrimination against immigrant workers, and environmental degradation, the capitalist class is powerless to stop the policies toward state neoliberalism.

Nevertheless, the transition from neoliberalism to state neoliberalism took the form of a transition, not the form of a rupture or a revolution. The transition took a fairly long period of time and it was a gradual, adaptive process without a clear blueprint. The reforms have proceeded by trial and error, with frequent mid-course corrections and reversal of policy. In other words, Chinese state developmental policies were not accomplished in "one bang", but are an ongoing process with many midcourse adjustments.

Situated in East Asia, China has long been attracted to the developmental state model that has achieved a remarkable post-war economic growth in South Korea, Taiwan, and Japan. Thus, Chang Kyung-Sup (2007) points out that there has been a conscious process of learning and transplanting technologies, industrial organization, and state policies among the East Asian states, and China is a leading example of this.

The rest of the book will examine how the communist party-state has restructured classes and redefined the pattern class conflicts among the capitalists, the workers, the peasants, and the middle class in post-socialist China. The next chapter will examine the dramatic comeback of the capitalist class in socialist China.

Chapter 4

THE MAKING OF A
CADRE–CAPITALIST CLASS

INTRODUCTION

During the Cultural Revolution, the Chinese capitalist class was the target of revolutionary attack. The following passage in *Quotations from Chairman Mao Tsetung* (Mao, 1972, pp. 17–19) was often used to justify the attack:

> In China, although in the main socialist transformation has been completed with respect to the system of ownership...there is still a bourgeoisie, and the remolding of the petty bourgeoisie has only just started. The class struggle is by no means over. The class struggle between the proletariat and the bourgeoisie...will continue to be long and tortuous and at times will even become very acute... We still have to wage a protracted struggle against bourgeois and petty-bourgeois ideology.

The following slogans were often shouted during the Cultural Revolution campaigns: "Crush the counter-attacks of the bourgeois reactionary line! Crush bourgeois economism! Long live the dictatorship of the proletariat! Long live the ever-victorious thought of Mao Tse-tung!" (Robinson, 1970, p. 122).

In post-socialist China since 1978, however, the capitalist class has staged a dramatic comeback. Yang Jinfu, the chief executive of his own chemical research firm, remarks, "In the past, we were con-

51

sidered traitors. Now, when government officials see me, they call me 'Yang Laoban' [Boss Yang], and they tell me the more money you make, the more glory you deserve (*Los Angeles Times*, July 3, 2001). On the occasion of the 80th anniversary of the Chinese Communist Party (CCP) in 2001, General Secretary Jiang Zemin even urged the party to recruit more "politically progressive" people from the private sector, because these people represent the interests of the advanced productive force (*China News Digest*, July 3, 2001). Jing Shuping, who heads China's top business association representing 27 million private business owners, has appealed for China's constitution to be amended to introduce rights for private business ownership.

This chapter will examine the dramatic rebirth and the remaking of the capitalist class in the post-socialist China. In particular, it will examine the origins, the characteristics, the transformation, and the impact of the capitalist class on China's development.

In the China field, there is no shortage of studies focusing on the capitalist class. However, these studies tend to focus on two issues. First, they examine the question of economic development: Has the existence of a capitalist class promoted or retarded China's economic development? He Qinglian (2000) is highly critical of those officials who strip off valuable state assets and invest them in the private sector; this cadre–capitalist class is seen as a parasitic class, engaged in rent seeking and corruption, blocking economic reforms and retarding China's economic development. On the other hand, Jane Duckett (2001) is impressed by the entrepreneurialism of bureaucrats who set up new profitable, risk-taking businesses. Instead of rent seeking, she argues, these cadre–capitalists are engaging in productive investment in a competitive market and helping to promote China's economic development.

Second, they focus on the democratization question: Will the capitalist class emerge as a force promoting democratization and civil society in China? Although White *et al.* (1996) see the potential for the capitalist class to nourish the seeds of civil society and democratization, many researchers (Pearson, 1998; Wank, 1995; Unger, 2006) argue that the capitalist class is either apolitical or has endorsed the existing status quo. They are highly skeptical that the capitalist class can play the role it historically has played elsewhere in bringing democratization to China.

Although these studies have enhanced our understanding of the cadre–capitalists, they do not examine them from a class perspective. Consequently, this chapter adopts E. P. Thompson's historical analysis to examine the dynamic processes of class formation, class conflict, and the ever-changing relationship between classes on the one hand and the state on the other hand. Such a historical class analysis approach helps to raise additional questions relevant to the study of Chinese capitalists. First, *the class boundary questions*: Where should researchers draw the boundary of the capitalist class? Who belongs to the capitalist class and who does not? For example, Margaret Pearson (1998) focuses on the owners of private enterprises and managers of foreign businesses operating in China, while Dorothy Solinger (1992) has broadened her scope to stress the bonding and incipient interpenetration between bureaucrats and merchants. Second, *the social origin questions*: From what social classes or groups do Chinese capitalists come from? Is there continuity or discontinuity between the old capitalist class of the early years of the PRC and that of the post-reform era? Third, *the class formation questions:* Has a capitalist class already been formed or is it still in the process of formation? What social, economic, and political activities does the capitalist class aspire to participate? Will the capitalist class be an ascending class in "socialist" China? Finally, *the class conflict questions*: In what ways have economic reforms triggered class differentiation, class polarization, and class conflict in Chinese society? What is the pattern of class conflict directed against the capitalist class and how does the capitalist class fight back against these offensives?

To deal with the above questions, the following sections will first examine the destruction and recreation of China's capitalist class over the past five decades. It will then examine two different routes in the making of the capitalist class: the embourgeoisement of cadres and the patronization of capitalists. Through these two different routes, this chapter argues, a cadre–capitalist class has emerged, which monopolizes economic capital, political capital, and social/network capital in Chinese society. The rest of this chapter then examines the class struggles against this nascent cadre–capitalist class, and how cadre–capitalists have striven for legitimization through reinventing themselves as entrepreneurs and incorporating themselves into the state bureaucracy.

THE DESTRUCTION AND RECREATION OF THE CAPITALIST CLASS: 1950s–1980s

A totally new statist society emerged in China after the 1949 Communist Revolution. The CCP built up an all-powerful Leninist-state that had the capacity to impose state policies onto the Chinese society. In addition, the CCP carried out a socialist project to eliminate the economic foundation of classes, so societal forces could be directly under the control of the state. The hostility from the U.S. during the Cold War, the forced withdrawal from the capitalist world-economy, and the constant threat of counter-revolutionaries made the CCP determined to try out its radical socialist experiment.

At the height of the Cultural Revolution, the capitalist class was singled out as the number one enemy of the Chinese people, and the Revolution was defined as a life-and-death class struggle between proletarian revolutionaries and capitalists/"capitalist roaders". After going through nationalization and the Cultural Revolution, the economic foundations and the political capacity of the capitalist class were largely eroded. As a result, the capitalist class was deprived of power/status/wealth in the society.

When the so-called "reformers" changed path and started a Four Modernizations program to jump-start the Chinese economy, they recreated a mixed economy composed of different states, collectives, and private sectors. The China Studies' literature tends to label this period as the era of market transition. However, although marketization has been a very important process in this period, one also should not overlook the profound transformations in spheres of production and ownership relations and the consequent re-emergence of classes and class conflicts. Reintegration into the capitalist world-economy has laid the economic foundations for the recreation of a foreign capitalist class engaging either in sole ownership of businesses on Chinese territory or in joint ventures with Chinese enterprises. The expansion of the private sector has given rise to a petty-bourgeois class (owners of *getihu* employing fewer than eight workers) and to a capitalist class (entrepreneurs employing eight workers or more).

Rapid economic development and the expansion of the private sector have led researchers to speculate whether China is in the process of going through a bourgeois revolution, with the capitalist class getting stronger, assuming a more active role in civil society, wanting more freedom and autonomy in running the economy, and posing a political challenge to the party-state. During the 1989 democracy movement in Tiananmen Square, nascent capitalists joined forces with workers and intellectuals, pointing to the emergence of a common front to challenge the party-state. In 1989, private traders on motorbikes delivered messages, while large companies such as the Stone Group provided financial support to the protesters (Howell, 1998, pp. 56–80). Researchers in the early 1990s, therefore, had high hope for a bourgeois democratic revolution in China. However, as the following sections show, the emergence of the Chinese capitalist class since 1989 has followed a different path from its Western counterpart.

THE MAKING OF THE CAPITALIST CLASS (I): THE *EMBOURGEOISEMENT* OF CADRES

The capitalist class re-emerged in the post-1978 reform era was stamped with the trademark of the statist society. In this chapter, a capitalist is distinguished from a petty-bourgeoisie by the scale of their enterprise. While a petty-bourgeoisie (*getihu*) has fewer than eight employees, a capitalist (private enterprise or *siying qiyejia*) has eight employees or more.

In the early 1980s, becoming a capitalist was generally seen as politically dangerous, as Victor Nee (2000) reports:

> ...merchants were vulnerable to the criticism that they were immoral in profiting from others' efforts without producing

anything themselves. Another common characterization of the new entrepreneur held that "If a person gets rich, there must have been something he did that was underhanded". According to one report, widely held negative stereotypes led entrepreneurs to feel that they were victims of "discrimination, sarcasm, and even attack". These stereotypes characterized entrepreneurs as "complex or mixed elements", "shady character", "people who engaged in crooked ways and dishonest practices, in gambling and speculation, and in making ill-gotten gains".

It was not until 1988 that the National People's Congress approved the establishment of "private enterprises" (*siying qiye*) with more than eight employees. Even then, the mere existence of formal legislation governing the private sector had not insulated it from broader shifts in the political environment. Kellee Tsai (2005) points out periodic political campaigns against spiritual pollution in 1983 and against bourgeois liberalization in 1987 had challenged the legitimacy of the capitalist class to varying degree.

Since the old capitalist class had been eliminated and discredited during the 1950s–1970s, an entirely new capitalist class had to be recreated in order to promote market reforms. The first path toward recreation, which can be called the *embourgeoisement* of cadres, has gone through the following processes.

Local State Corporatism in Rural China

During the first decade of the economic reforms in the 1980s, rural cadres turned local state enterprises into profitable township and other collective enterprises (local state corporatism), and developed joint ventures with foreign capitalists and overseas Chinese capitalists (Oi, 1995). Some even quit their official positions, set up village enterprises, and hired their kin and friends to run them. Since cadres possessed the political capital as well as the social networks necessary to run collective and private enterprises, they had an edge over other groups in taking advantages of nascent business opportunities in rural China in the first decade of the reform era (Goodman, 1996).

Corporatization of Urban State Enterprises

During the second stage of urban reform in the mid-1990s, when the state called for the corporatization of state enterprises through shareholding, a massive diversion occurred of the assets of state enterprises into the private hands of the cadres in charge of them. Since some companies set the face value of their stock incredibly cheaply and sold stock exclusively to cadres, senior cadres directly in charge of corporation reforms often became large shareholders overnight (Ding, 1999).

The aim of corporatization has been to transform state enterprises into purely profit-making companies, thereby nullifying their character as socialist institutions. The state's plan is gradually to divest itself of all except the 3,000 largest and most important state-owned enterprises. The smaller state-owned enterprises will be allowed to merge, go bankrupt, sell stakes to their employees, or, as is now increasingly common, be bought by the cadres who managed them (Hjellum, 2000; Huchet, 2000). However, for the largest 3,000 state-owned enterprises in such strategic industries as oil, steel, mining, telecommunications, shipping, and banking, the party-state will still own, manage, and tightly regulate them for the sake of national security.

State Entrepreneurship

The late 1990s started the so-called "state entrepreneurship" (the engaging in private businesses by cadres). Ding Xueliang's studies (2000a, 2000b) point to three ways through which cadres can transform state enterprise properties into private business resources: organizational proliferation, consortium-building, and the strategy of "one manager, two businesses".

Organizational proliferation in state firms can take various forms. Cadres can strip off the enterprise's best-equipped or most profitable segments and turn these into new collective-owned companies; they can split the state firm *per se* into multiple corporate bodies across several industrial lines; or they can allocate its productive assets to the relatives of the firm's employees, who set themselves up as subcontractors. In all these instances, the original state firm is kept alive on paper even though it has ceased working in the normal sense.

Consortium-building (*lianying*) is an inter-firm arrangement similar in nature to a joint venture: a partnership between Chinese bodies in which a state-owned enterprise sets up a new firm in collaboration with a non-state-owned enterprise or with a non-commercial unit such as an official women's association, a school, or a hospital. Ding Xueliang (2000b) reports that a third of the major consortia organized from Beijing are situated in Shenzhen, which is among the least regulated precincts in the country. State-owned enterprises prefer grafting onto collective, rural, private firms, or joint ventures; by doing so, they obscure their public nature and water down their state-owned character.

The *one manager, two businesses* strategy involves cadres in departments within the state administration setting up profit-seeking businesses in the private sector to earn income for themselves. Staff members are gradually transferred out of the state administration and into the private businesses. The new private businesses thus help relieve the financial problems of the state departments as well as providing employment opportunities for cadres. Although these activities are not strictly illegal, they are neither officially permitted nor encouraged by the central government. However, Jane Duckett (2001) labels these activities as "entrepreneurial" because these businesses are productive (they build buildings, produce goods, provide catering services, trade in commodities, etc.) in a competitive market, because they employ some of their own staff, and because they generate profits for their units. Due to their involvement in private businesses, these cadres are now no longer just plan implementers, but also capitalists.

Corinna-Barbara Francis (2001) points out that the above three "entrepreneurial" practices are carried out by all sorts of state entities: "local and municipal governments, national ministries, the army, national and local public security bureaus, party organizations, universities, scientific institutes many of which have become profit-seeking market actors who run their own often extensive business empire". The army, for example, has become one of China's largest business conglomerates, running a sprawling business empire with interests in manufacturing, transportation, import–export trade, entertainment, and tourism; it also operates some of the largest corporations in Hong Kong. The coexistence and interpenetration of various forms of ownership between the state and non-state domains have provided a golden opportunity for cadres to transform themselves into capitalist owners and managers of semi-state, collective, and private properties.

A series of revealing inquiries into the Chinese party-state have been published by *Bloomberg News, the Wall Street Journal* and *the New York Times* in 2012 to document the marriage between wealth and power in China. Of particular interests are the so-called "princelings": sons, daughters, and grandchildren of the revolutionary founders who fought along Mao Zedong and stood with Deng Xiaoping. The children seem to have inherited a golden touch. Bloomberg reported in December 26, 2012 on the fortunes of 103 descendents of the revolutionaries revered in China as the "Eight Immortals", who backed Deng two years after Mao's death. Three of the descendents headed or still head state-owned companies with combined assets of US$1.6 trillion in 2011, or about a fifth of China's national output. About 26 ran or held positions in state-owned companies; 43 ran their own business or became executives in private firms (The Editorial Board, 2013).

THE MAKING OF THE CAPITALIST CLASS (II): THE PATRONIZATION OF CAPITALISTS

The second way toward the creation of a capitalist class has been through cadre patronage of capitalists. Nascent mainland capitalists, as well as overseas Chinese capitalists from Hong Kong and Taiwan, in many cases have found themselves still too weak to challenge outdated bureaucratic rules and regulations, corruption, and irregular taxes. Instead of trying to transform the state bureaucracy or pushing for a more transparent regulatory system, most capitalists have preferred to work within the existing structure. In conditions where a comprehensive legal framework for private capital is lacking, the patronage of local cadres can provide business owners with a way to get around the vacuum of formal institutions. Local cadres, who now have a political mandate for economic development and for implementing a mixed planned/market economy, possess a great deal of power within their administrative jurisdictions. This power is expressed through discretionary decisions benefiting favored persons and through control over information about policy changes and policy implementation (Wu, 2001). Minglu Chen (2011) points out that the capitalist still needs to depend on the local government and its officials for the development of their businesses, as the latter control resources, loans, and some raw materials, and is an important source of business information and business contacts.

Informal Patronage by Local Cadres

What capitalists needed was to find a cadre patron to provide them with vital information, to get them access to credit, raw materials, and markets, and to shield them from arbitrary and irregular taxes. A Taiwanese capitalist made the following comment on the situation in the Pearl River Delta:

> We have to maintain good connections with the people in the tax bureau and customs. Low-level officials are especially troublemakers. As we understand it, there is a difference between breaking the rules and breaking the law. We are not perfect. They can always find faults with our business. They come to talk about a lot of irrelevant things. But the words imply more than is evident at face value. They merely want to get surcharges and fines, or bribes (Wu, 2001, p. 38).

The support of a cadre patron can also help capitalists avoid the labor regulations that apply in the state sector so as to save on the additional costs of pension schemes, health and welfare insurance, and environmental protection facilities. As Margaret Pearson (1998, p. 115) remarks, "For private entrepreneurs, ties with local cadres are absolutely necessary to their success".

In order to gain the support of their patrons, capitalists have mobilized social networks, kinship ties, and overseas connections, and have provided their patrons with material and symbolic gifts and processing fees. In return, cadre patrons favor their clientele capitalists over other non-clientele capitalists. Patron–client ties have been pervasive in the reform era between small capitalists and local cadres staffing the state's administrative, distributive, and productive organs (Wu, 2001; Goodman, 2000; Hjellum, 2000).

Formal Patronage by Local Party-State

Nascent capitalists seeking to move up to the big time and to expand continuously frequently adopt a strategy of formal patronage by registering their private companies as collective enterprises (a practice called *wearing a red hat*). The collective sector thus includes a whole series of enterprises that are the product of capitalist–cadre cooperation. Estimates on privately-owned collective enterprises range from one-third nationally to as high as 90% in some localities (Tsai, 2005, p. 1136).

To qualify for collective standing, capitalists offer shares and partial ownership to their cadre patrons. David Goodman (1996, pp. 222–223) explains that "the political reasons were relatively obvious and could be regarded at the time as a form of insurance policy against any further change of mind by the CCP. Economically, there is a better tax environment for collective than private-sector enterprises, and land and labor could be provided in cooperation with local government."

Formal Patronage by Central Party-State

The latest development in the legitimization of capitalists has been their recruitment into the Communist Party. In August 1989, soon after the democratic protests in Tiananmen Square, the Communist

Party imposed a ban on recruiting the capitalist class into the organization on the ground that private businessmen were "exploiters" and that allowing them to join the party would change its nature.

However, as Dickson (2004, p. 251) explains, local officials had an incentive to reach out to entrepreneurs even if central leaders disapproved. Creating economic growth is a key criterion for career advancement, and throughout the 1990s most economic growth and job creation came from the private sector. Therefore, local officials began to recruit successful entrepreneurs into the party despite of the formal ban. The percentage of private entrepreneurs who were communist party members (a group known as *red capitalists*) grew from around 13% in 1993 to more than 20% in 2000.

Facing this unstoppable recruitment drive of local officials, the Central government finally gave in and lifted the ban on recruiting entrepreneurs into the Party. At the CCP's 80th anniversary on July 1, 2001, Jiang Zemin, the General Secretary of the Communist Party, presented a new *Three Represents* policy to urge the communist party to recruit more "politically progressive" people from the private sector, saying that entrepreneurs, owners of private enterprises, and employees of foreign firms who "make contributions to developing socialism's productive forces and its other endeavors through honest labor and work" should be given a chance to join the communist party. On July 2, 2001, *Renmin Ribao* further explained that "as a result of economic reforms, individual wealth and living standards of most of the Chinese people have continued to rise. In this situation, it is too simplistic to use levels of wealth to judge whether a person is politically progressive or backward. Instead, it is important to examine the person's concrete political thinking and behavior, to see how a person acquires and manages wealth, and to see whether a person's labor has made any contribution to the Chinese socialist economy."

Dickson (2004, p. 251) presents the following figures: at the 2003 National People's Congress, 55 entrepreneurs were selected as deputies. Entrepreneurs have been asked to serve in local legislatures in even larger numbers: over 17% of the entrepreneurs belong to local people's congress, and 35% belong to local people's political consultative conferences, a body designed to allow discussion between the party and other local elites.

Among China's richest 1,024 people, *Wall Street Journal* reported in 2012 that 160 are seated in the Communist Party Congress or in a prominent advisory group. The business card of one clothing magnate listed 10 political positions (The Editorial Board, 2013).

Recruitment of capitalists into the communist party has solidified the bond between cadres and capitalists. Previously, the traffic ran only one way, with cadres transforming themselves into capitalists: tens of thousands of party members have been involved in businesses as managers of state enterprises, organizations that have been privatized, organizations that have split from their parent companies, and shareholding companies that are run commercially with the state maintaining a share. With the new "Three Represents" policy in 2001, a reverse flow has begun, transforming capitalists into party members and cadres.

THE FORMATION OF A HYBRID CADRE–CAPITALIST CLASS

Cadre–Capitalists

Due to the prevalence of the above two mechanisms, emerging state–capitalist relations are characterized by the fusion of the *political capital* of the cadres, the *economic capital* of the capitalists, and the *social/network capital* embedded in local society. Many collective enterprises are owned and run by capitalists, while many private enterprises are spun off of state properties owned and run by cadres or their kin. Garcia *et al.* (2011) show that families play an important role in the emergence of the cadre–capitalist class because they found many capitalists are former cadres or are the relatives of cadres. This fusion of forms makes it very hard to distinguish what in the private sector is owned by the state, by collectives, or by capitalists, because the boundaries of their property relations are often blurred.

The fusion of forms has also eroded the distinction between cadres and capitalists. On the one hand, cadres often engage in capitalist activities in the private sector while employed by the state, thereby benefiting from their political connections and preferential access to resources, capital, technology, and licenses. On the other hand, capitalists in the private sector enjoy greater access, through their cadre patrons, to political power than in the Maoist period (Francis, 2001). These fuzzy property boundaries and blurring of the distinction between cadres and capitalists have created a powerful hybrid, which can be called a "cadre–capitalist" class.

David Goodman (2000, p. 15) reports that "most entrepreneurs, including those in the private sector of the economy…either had social origins in the party-state or were for the most part incorporated into its activities". Torstein Hjellum (2000, p. 119) reports a survey finding that "generally speaking, cadres — half government functionaries and half business managers — were at the core of the social networks of entrepreneurs in both cities and towns and rural areas … a good relationship with the government was an important prerequisite for having a satisfying income". Ching-Ching Ni (2001) reports that "as many as 42% of the private company heads in parts of Jiangsu and Zhejiang provinces, coastal areas that historically have been the cradles of Chinese private business, are also party members. In Shanghai, the number hovers around 13%. Some of them are also the party boss at their party branch". This hybrid cadre–capitalist class has monopolized political capital, economic capital, and social/network capital in Chinese society. Its members are the beneficiaries of the existing partial reforms, mixed economy, and hybrid ownership arrangements.

Class Formation

Although the capitalist class was almost nonexistent in the 1970s, it grew very fast in the post-1978 era during the rapid economic development in the transitional economy. In 2003, Kellee Tsai (2005, p. 1132) reports that there were 26.57 million private businesses, employing more than 200 million people and accounting for one-third of the GDP. Starting in the late 1990s, the capitalist class had become very active in social and economic activities. Members of this class have formed all sorts of class organizations, such as the All China Federation of Industry and Commerce, the China Enterprise Confederation, the China Enterprise Directors Association, the China Township and Village Enterprise Association, and the Chinese Foreign Sector Business Association. They have established an extensive organizational networks extending from the national to provincial, city, and county levels. Their associations hold annual meetings as well as special conferences, such as the China Enterprise Summit in Beijing in April 2001. Activities and speeches at the annual meeting and at special conferences are widely reported in such national newspapers as *Renmin Ribao*. They also have their own newspapers, such as *The Chinese Commercial Times.* They also donated money and materials up to 700,000,000 *yuan* to help the victims in the flooding region in 1998 (*People's Daily*, March 15, 1999). This kind of charity work is an important means for the nascent capitalist class to develop a positive image in Chinese society.

In addition, Scott Kennedy (2005) shows that a variety of business associations have sprung up in post-socialist China, often industry-specific, organized from bottom-up, and active at lobbying the state and in some cases unilaterally setting industry standards and regulations. These associations are most autonomous, more assertive, and less interested in simply representing the state's interests. However, Kennedy points out in the 1990s that these business associations tend to limit their activities to issues within the economic sphere and are not involved in larger public policy issues.

Furthermore, the capitalist class has begun to manifest a distinctive bourgeois lifestyle. Many large or medium Chinese cities now have luxurious neighborhoods, often guarded by state-of-the-art security systems. Consumption too is highly stratified. Specialty stores sell high-fashion items to the rich (He, 2000, p. 95). The following story reveals the conspicuous consumption pattern of the *nouveau riche*:

I do not wear the same outfit two days running. My favorite is a spring dress by a Japanese designer that cost 9,000 *yuan.* I buy my clothes in Hong Kong and Macau or the Printemps department store in Shanghai. I recently spent 20,000 *yuan* for an operation to lose weight. Whenever I go to Hong Kong, I spend $14,000 for half a kilogram of swallow's nest. I eat a little each morning for my health, and it lasts about two months (*SCMP*, March 27, 2001, p. 13).

The above story also reports that the *nouveau riche* sends their spouses or children abroad to obtain an education or a passport that will facilitate parking some assets abroad. In addition, Pogrebin (2011) reports that the new billionaires in China have developed a growing interest in Western as well as Asian art and they have become an increasing powerful force in the global art market, thus raising paddles for big-ticket artworks despite a backdrop of global economic turmoil.

By the late 1990s, members of the capitalist class were becoming more politically active, and they began to call for more representation in political bodies. For example, at the Summit of Chinese Enterprises on May 24, 2001, the delegates complained thus:

Although private entrepreneurs experience a lot of problems, they do not have many representatives in the central decision-making bodies. China has 1.4 million enterprises and 62 million entrepreneurs, but they have only 48 representatives in the National People of Congress and 46 representatives in the Political Consultation Committee. All successful entrepreneurs want more political representation. If they do not get sufficient protection or political representation, their enthusiasm will be low because they are worried that policy changes could suddenly happen any day. As a result, these most successfully entrepreneurs in China often invest their profits overseas, buy foreign stocks, or send their kids abroad for foreign education. (Available at http://www.cec-ceda.org.cn/yjbg/nw91-01/2001/y24.htm)

At the above summit, capitalists also issued a call: "[O]ur institution should be more open. The government needs to carry out political and economic protection as well as providing legal support, so that private entrepreneurs receive their fair share of their political status". In 1998, the government revised the constitution to protect private property from infringement, and Chinese capitalists continue to work hard to try to influence the government to serve their class interests. In 2001, business organizations have further appealed for China's constitution to be amended to introduce rights for private business ownership. It was proposed that the constitution should guarantee the absolute protection of all commercial assets and real estate in the private business sector (*SCMP*, July 20, 2001).

Due to this strong push by the business lobby, a new Property Law was passed by the National People's Congress in 2007. This Property Law guarantees equal legal protection to private property as to public property. Moreover, the Property Law also spells out specific protection to incomes, houses, and tools of production, investment and personal savings, prohibiting these properties from being seized, expropriated, or damaged by any groups or individuals.

However, despite its growing economic and social power and increasing political participation, this nascent cadre–capitalist class faces the serious challenge of legitimization.

CLASS CONFLICT

Class Differentiation and Class Polarization

Under the conditions described above, a class-divided society has quickly emerged in China. In the cities, a formerly relatively homogeneous urban population is now split into a capitalist class, an old middle class of the self-employed and small employers, and a working class subdivided into permanent urban workers and temporary migrant workers. In private and collective enterprises, temporary migrants often work in a situation similar to that of their European counterparts in the early stages of the Industrial Revolution. They have to work very long hours, get only minimum wages, must obey strict work discipline, are hired on a day-to-day basis, and are unable to form labor unions to protect their interests. Studies have shown that business owners frequently exploit factors of gender (paying female workers less than male workers), ethnicity (hiring out-of-province migrant workers rather than local workers), and kinship ties (recruiting workers from the same village as that of the foreman) in order to facilitate their control over the workers (Lee, 1998; Pun, 2001).

In addition, there is a growing trend toward class polarization. Many studies show that the rich are getting richer and the poor are getting poorer. At the top there are millionaires and even billionaires; at the bottom there is an underclass of temporary migrants in the cities, and poverty is widespread in inland provinces. In the early 1980s, China was among the world's most egalitarian societies. By the mid-1990s, the inequalities of income distribution in China already exceeded the inequality found not only in the transition economies of Eastern Europe and the high-income countries of Western Europe and North America, but also in China's Asian neighbors, such as India, Pakistan, and Indonesia (Wang and Hu, 1999).

In this situation, conflict has emerged, organized along class lines and raising class issues. In the countryside, many rural protests have occurred, with poor peasants complaining about high taxes, irregular taxes, low prices for their agricultural products, encroachment on their land and houses, the state's IOUs, and similar issues. In the cities, workers have protested their layoffs, the closing down of their enterprises, the reduction of their wages and benefits, abuses by their managers, and suchlike.

The Superimposition of Class Conflict

As a result of the above processes, class conflict in the post-1978 reform era has the potential to intensify. Different forms of class conflicts have been superimposed upon one another, resulting in attacks on the cadre–capitalist class from various classes. State workers have blamed the cadre–capitalist class for layoffs and reductions of benefits. Temporary migrant workers have blamed the cadre–capitalist class for preventing them from settling in the cities and market towns. Peasants have blamed the cadre–capitalist class for increasing taxes, taking away their land, and imposing a coercive one-child policy. The new middle class has blamed the cadre–capitalist class for their relative decline in living standards and repressive working environments.

The monopolization of political capital, economic capital, and social/network capital by cadre–capitalists has made this class highly vulnerable to attacks by other classes. Very often, this cadre–capitalist class has been seen to be corrupt, extravagant, morally wrong, abusive of its power, and exploitative of societal resources for the purposes of self-enrichment. Various labels, such as "parvenus", "upstarts", "crony capitalism", "power capital", "rent seeking", "bureaucratic capitalism", and "primitive accumulation" have been used to condemn cadre–capitalists. Often, an instinctive reaction is to attribute individual economic wealth solely to official corruption or other illegal arrangements. As An Chen (2002, p. 412) laments, "A large portion, if not a majority, of the bourgeois have prospered from the commercial privileges deriving from political lineage. They are essentially a parasitic appendage of corrupt and unrestricted political power and have a taken-for-granted personal stake in preventing regime change". Thus, the involvement of cadres with private business activities is often judged as either criminal or unacceptable (Goodman, 1996, p. 227).

The following message in the popular magazine *Southern Weekly* is illustrative of the general sentiment of the Chinese society: "Highly officials are buddies to big money; big money is a buddy to high officials. The grassroots population totally condemns such behavior. Legally speaking, those who committed the crimes must be prosecuted according to the law. Morally speaking, such crimes outrageously violate trust in the government by common citizens, worsening the moral standard of the whole society" (*Southern Weekly*, July 27, 2001). Furthermore, the public is highly cynical about official campaigns against corruption, as these campaigns are no longer seen as threats to corruption, but rather as instruments of political leverage and blackmail for further personal gain (He, 2000, p. 72).

In China's newspapers and magazines, for example, cadres' engagement in private business activities is seen as "rent-seeking" activity, an exchange between wealth and power. On the one hand, the wealthy benefit from "giving out a chicken and getting back a cow". On the other hand, powerful officials benefit from bribery. Political rent making is the process through which state officials use administrative means (such as double price systems, tariffs, quotas, special policies, etc.) to increase their personal wealth as well as the wealth of capitalists. These condemnations suggest that corruption is so widespread that many local party-state officials have lost the trust of the Chinese grassroots population.

In the late 2010s, a new term called *the black collar class* is used in the Chinese mass media to describe the behavior of this cadre–capitalist class. They are labeled as the black collar class because their clothes are black, their cars are black, their income is hidden, their life is hidden, and their work is hidden. Their houses overlook the best landscape in the quietest location, they play golf, travel at public expenses, and enjoy a life of luxury. This mysterious social group is said to be the most shameless group in the world because they use the party-state apparatus to illegally appropriate wealth for themselves (China Translated, 2009).

BOURGEOIS STRUGGLES

Ideological Struggles through Reinventing Themselves as Loyal "Entrepreneurs"

To fight back against these condemnations, members of the cadre–capitalist class have worked hard to reinvent themselves over the past few years. First, these individuals have labeled themselves as "entrepreneurs", rather than "capitalists". It has been important that the old "capitalist" label be dropped, as this label was totally discredited during the Maoist period. The adoption of the new label of "entrepreneur" thus has helped capitalists to reinvent themselves. A report in *Renmin Ribao,* for example, stresses that an entrepreneur is not an ordinary manager of production. Instead, he is a kind of special human capital. He is a very scarce resource, and he occupies an important position in the productive forces. Entrepreneurship thus should be seen as incorporating a capacity for leadership, a capacity to make coordinated decisions, a capacity to innovate, and a capacity to seize opportunities.

Second, capitalists claim that their entrepreneurship and expertise are indispensable to China's economic development. The *Market Newspaper* (September 16, 2000) points out that since the economy is at the center of the contemporary world, since the economy is built on enterprises, and since entrepreneurs are the soul of enterprises, national economic competition is actually competition among national entrepreneurs. Therefore, if the Chinese government wants to enhance its competitive strengthen in the global economy, it needs to create a better environment for the Chinese entrepreneurs to realize their potential.

Third, capitalists stress their loyalty to the Chinese nation and to the Communist Party. At the National Entrepreneur Activity Day on April 21, 1995, one speech stressed that the goal of socialist entrepreneurs is to develop the national economy. A socialist entrepreneur should aim to serve the people, to bring prestige to the Chinese nation, to correctly carry out the Communist Party's directives and policies, and to serve the people wholeheartedly (Available at http://www.cec-ceda.org.cn/body/talk/ybh/ybh-7.htm).

Fourth, instead of boasting about their wealth, capitalists present to the public a picture of much lower incomes than their counterparts in big American and Japanese corporations. In China, entrepreneurs receive only 2–3 times the income received by average workers. By contrast, in 1997 the average income of a senior manager in American corporations was 326 times more than the average salary. Furthermore, a 1999 survey of Chinese enterprises revealed that 63% of employees of state enterprises received a salary of less than 20,000 *yuan* a year; by contrast, 50% of employees of collective enterprises, and 80% of employees of private enterprises, earned more than 20,000 *yuan* a year (Available at http://www.cec-ceda.org.cn/yjbg/baog/jiakuai2.htm).

Finally, capitalists have emphasized that it is not easy to set up new enterprises during a period of transition from a planned economy to a socialist market economy. Entrepreneurs have faced a variety of challenges in getting capital, managing a workforce that has not previously been penalized for inefficiency, and meeting changing market demands. Capitalists have worked very hard to overcome these challenges, and feel that they receive insufficient rewards for their significant contributions to China. Therefore, capitalists are asking for more honor, higher status, better working conditions, and more comfortable living arrangements. They want the Chinese government to develop encouragement mechanisms to recognize their contributions by giving them more spiritual and material rewards.

Political Corporatism

Another mechanism for legitimization of capitalists is political corporatism. Capitalist organizations, such as the All China Federation of Industry and Commerce and the Private Business Association, have worked hard to gain formal state endorsement and to be formally included in the state bureaucracy in order to be accepted as legitimate organizations in society.

The constitutions of these capitalist organizations aptly show their subordination to the state. For example, the first item of the constitution of the All-China Federation of Industry and Commerce (ACFIC), entitled "General Principles", states that "(the) ACFIC is a civil association organized by Chinese industrial and commercial groups under the leadership of the CCP. It serves as a bridge and a conveyor belt between the party-state and persons in the non-state sector. It is an assistant helping the state to manage the non-state sector". The constitution of the China Township and Village Enterprise Association states that the association's major task is "to develop a bridging function between the township and village enterprises and the government, and to propagate the government's directives, policies, and laws, as well as to convey the demands and situations of enterprises to the government and to help protect the legal interests of enterprises" (Available at http://www.sunground. net/xqxh.htm).

Although under the control of the state, capitalist organizations still play an important role as advocates for new business interests. In return for their acceptance of the state's authority, these new class organizations are granted privileges that gain them access to the state. Margaret Pearson (1998, p. 270) points out that these organizations have helped capitalists with arbitration and coordinated businesses' ties with government agencies. They also claim to pass complaints of businesses upward to relevant government authorities, and in some cases they have successfully influenced the state's policy toward business, although usually in narrow areas and at the local level. In addition, they have penetrated the state bureaucracy and obtained preferential access to state resources, capital, loans, materials, information, and bureaucratic licenses (Francis, 2001, p. 281).

Struggles to Protect its Class Interests

After securing the supports of the party-state, the capitalist class is strong enough to engage in struggles with other classes. In 2008, the Chinese capitalist class rallied against the legislation of the new Labor Contract Law. A leading voice among the Chinese capitalist class was Ms. Zhang Yin, who was the chairwoman of Hong Kong-listed Nine Dragon Paper Holdings, the largest containerboard manufacturer in China. Zhang was reported as the richest woman in China in 2006 and became a member of Chinese People's Political Consultative Committee (CPPCC) in 2008. In attacking the draft Labor Contract Law, Zhang said that "if the law over protects the labor, an enterprise can hardly operate" (World by Data, 2007). Zhang further complained that "signing labor contracts without a fixed-term proposed in the new Labor Contract Law is equal to the return to the 'iron rice bowl' policy during the age of planned economy" (*China Review News*, 2008). Later at the CPPCC meeting in March 2008, Zhang made a motion calling for the scrapping of the core provision of the Labor Contract Law, i.e., eliminating the provision that long-time workers who had provided a substantial service to an employer should receive an open-ended labor contract. Zhang's CPPCC motion had attracted mass media attention and aroused national heated debates on how to enhance labor protection in order to avoid "potential hazards" to the local economy.

In late 2010s, foreign businesses in China voiced their frustration over China's heavily regulated market — a bureaucratic maze many transnational capitalists say was designed deliberately to hamstring non-Chinese players to the advantage of their local competitors (Ford, 2010). European Union Chamber of Commerce in China also issued a position paper listing hundreds of market-access problems of foreign companies across a range of industries. Foreign companies also complained loudly that they are being shut out much of the lucrative government procurement sector. For example, not one of the 25 valuable contracts awarded to companies under the Chinese government's US$586 billion stimulus program went to a foreign-owned company (Jiang, 2010).

Despite the strong protests from the transnational capitalist class, China's strategic industries remained highly regulated. Instead of market liberalization, there was a huge expansion of the state sector at the expense of the private sector, aptly expressed in the catchphrase *guo jin, min tui* or "the state advances, the private sector retreats". During 2008–2009, investments by state-controlled companies skyrocketed, driven by hundreds of billions of dollars of government spending and state bank lending to combat the global financial crisis.

There are no comprehensive statistics to catalog the expansion of the state's influence on the economy, so the shift is partly inferred from such coarse measures as the share of financing in the economy provided by state banks (which sharply rose during the financial crisis); the list of the 100 largest publicly-listed Chinese companies, all but one of which are majority state owned; or the growing political and financial influences of China's state-owned giants — 129 huge conglomerates that answer directly to the central government, and thousands of smaller ones run by the provinces and cities (Wines, 2010a).

While no public breakdown exists, most expert say that the vast bulk of the 4 trillion renminbi (US$586 billion) stimulus package in 2008 that China pumped out for new highways, railroads, and other big projects went to state-owned companies. Some of the largest state companies used the flood of money to strengthen their dominance in their current market or to enter new ones. Wines (2010a) reports that "some of the upstream state-owned enterprises are now expanding downstream, organizing themselves as vertical units. They are just operating on a much larger scale".

CONCLUSION

This chapter has examined the making of the cadre–capitalist class in China. Using a historical class analysis, this chapter has shown that the legacies of the Cultural Revolution and a strong Leninist party-state have played a decisive role in the making of the capitalist class. Since the economic foundations and political capacity of the capitalist class were completely eroded during the Maoist period, the old capitalist class was not able to seize the opportunity of the post-1978 economic reforms to revitalize itself. As a result, an *embourgeoisement of cadres* has taken place through the processes of local state corporatism, corporatization of state enterprises, and cadre engagement in private businesses. At the same time, nascent capitalists outside the bureaucracy have needed cadre patrons, not only to help them to get access to market and bank loans but also to fend off the predatory activities of corrupt cadres. Through the processes of embourgeoisement of cadres and the *patronization of capitalists*, a fusion of political capital, economic capital, and social/network capital in local society has taken place, leading to a formation of a powerful cadre–capitalist class. By the late 1990s, the cadre–capitalist class had begun to take visible form, exhibiting a lifestyle of conspicuous consumption, establishing class organizations at the national, provincial, and local class levels, and starting to call for constitutional revision and more political representation in order to expand their class interests. Nevertheless, the formation of the cadre–capitalist class has occurred side by side with growing class differentiation, class polarization, and class conflict. Consequently, class conflict has emerged, with cadre–capitalists being challenged by almost all other classes. Cadre–capitalists have been attacked as corrupt, rent seeking, selfish, abusive of their political power, and wasteful of the country's economic resources for private conspicuous consumption. In the battle for legitimization, cadre–capitalists have tried to reinvent themselves as hard-working, nationalistic entrepreneurs and have developed a close working relationship with the party-state through political incorporation.

As the above summary shows, the pattern of emergence of the cadre–capitalist class in post-reform China has been quite different from the historical experience of Western Europe, Russia and Eastern Europe, or third world countries. In Western Europe, the emergence of a new capitalist class led to the expansion of the public sphere and civil society, eventually leading to a bourgeois democratic revolution that overthrew the old feudal order. In China, on the other hand, the emergence of the cadre–capitalist class has posed no challenge to the status quo. Since the cadre–capitalists have decided to cooperate with and work inside the party-state, it is unlikely that this class will serve as a motivating force for a classical bourgeois democratic revolution in China.

In Russia and Eastern Europe, former cadres have often engaged in corruption, rent seeking, and stripping off of the assets of state enterprises, leading to the decline of these national economies. But in China, although cadre–capitalists have also turned public assets into private property, many of their investments are in productive, profitable enterprises in a competitive market. While it is true that corporatization and engagement in businesses have greatly enriched the cadres, their productive investments have also played an important role in promoting economic development, leading to a very remarkable growth rate in the 1990s, even in the shadow of the Asian financial crisis.

In third world countries which adopted statist development policies, state bureaucrats have targeted industry, providing incentives such as subsidies and lower tax rates, and monitor corporations' performance. Although these developmental states take an active role in governing the market, they usually have not engaged directly in businesses. The case in China is quite different: Chinese cadres have seized the golden opportunity of economic reform, have made use of their political connections and management skills, and have turned themselves into owners and managers in the private sector. Since the boundary between state enterprises and collective/private enterprises is fuzzy, it is immensely difficult to draw a class boundary between cadres and capitalists in China. This cadre–capitalist class is hence a unique hybrid, with a leg each in both the state and the private sectors. Using only the classical Marxist definition of economic ownership to define this class would certainly miss out its distinctive hybrid characteristics.

What is the future of this cadre–capitalist class? Several possible scenarios exist. First, the cadre–capitalists could turn into *an ascending class*. In this scenario, the Chinese economy keeps on expanding, and the Chinese government successfully solves the challenges of class conflict through the establishment of new welfare packages and more humane labor laws to protect the workers, the eradication of widespread corruption, and initiation of some kinds of democratic elections. In this scenario, decreasing class conflict and rapid economic development might help to enhance the status of cadre–capitalists. They could be seen as nationalistic entrepreneurs making significant contributions to the Chinese economy and society.

Second, the cadre–capitalists could follow the path of *a descending class*. In this scenario, the Chinese economy is in trouble, due to negative economic growth, massive unemployment, and increasing poverty triggered by the downward turn of the capitalist world-economy in the early 21st century. Growing class polarization leads to the intensification of class conflict. Corruption remains acute, and the cadre–capitalist class is blamed for the depressed situation in the Chinese economy and society. Its status falls and its privileges are strongly contested by other classes.

Finally, there is the path of *segmentation*. In this scenario, after most state enterprises have completed their corporatization, after cadres have completely gained control of the ownership and management of the private businesses they have set up unofficially, after

China's constitution has guaranteed the '"sacredness" of private property, after the legal system has clarified the boundary of state enterprises and private enterprises, and after capitalist organizations have been empowered to protect and expand their class interests independent of the state, it may be to the capitalist class's advantage to sever its links to the state bureaucracy in order to fully reap the benefits of their ownership and control of private enterprises. This de-linking with the state bureaucracy could enhance the capitalists' claim that they are no longer corrupted cadres. Instead, they are truly nationalistic entrepreneurs making significant contributions to the Chinese economy and society.

Since the cadre–capitalist class is still at the early stages of its formation, its future is still in flux. At present, this class is still too weak to make its own history and promote the classical bourgeois democratic revolution. Its future development depends very much on the contours of the Chinese economy and the party-state in 21st century.

Chapter 5

THE TRANSFORMATION
OF THE MAOIST WORKING CLASS
IN URBAN CHINA

THE MAOIST WORKING CLASS DURING 1950s–1960s

In the first half of the 20th century, China's working class suffered from a fate common to their counterparts in the third world countries: Job tenure was unstable, labor turnover was high, and the numbers of unemployed continually swelled by the migration from rural areas. Wages were at a level that guaranteed poverty and welfare provisions too were nonexistent. Most of the Chinese workers were craftsmen working in tiny workshops and labor legislation was either nonexistent or weak at best (Chesneaux, 1968).

However, the Chinese Communist Revolution drastically transformed the nature of Chinese working class in the 1950s. First, the speed of the making of the modern Chinese working class was unprecedented. While it took decades, if not centuries, for the formation of working class during the Industrial Revolution in Western European countries, the Chinese working class was created in only eight years. After the Communist Revolution in 1949, there was very rapid growth of a modern industrial sector of large enterprises, especially in the industrial Northeast. It took the communist party-state only eight years (1949–1957) to transform privately-owned enterprises into state enterprises and combine the massive sector of small workshops into cooperatives or small, state-run factories

79

(Walder, 1984). In the 1950s, therefore, we observed the historical transformation of the working class dominated by traditional craftsmen working in small workshops to one dominated by modern workers in large-scale manufacturing employment. The size of the Chinese working class expanded enormously in the 1950s as the party-state began a rapid industrialization drive in the heavy industry. This "quick transition" enabled the Chinese working class to skip the craft-industrial stage through which their Western counterparts had gone through the painful process of capital–labor conflict, collective bargaining, strikes, etc.

Second, as Walder (1984) points out, the nature of the proletarianization process in China was different from that in the West. In Western Europe, proletarianization involved an expropriation process in which the peasantry in the countryside lost the control of the means of production, got thrown out of the peasant community, and were forced to migrate long-distance to the cities to seek a living as wage laborers. Thus, Western proletarianization happened side by side with urbanization when a rural peasant was turned into an urban worker.

In contrast, China had a surplus population both in the cities and in the countryside. China already had an extensive network of large cities and a large densely populated rural population supported by a highly productive, labor-intensive system of agriculture. Moreover, the Chinese population was growing at an increasing rate in the 1950s after the end of World War II and the Civil War.

Therefore, in order to prevent rural-to-urban migration from swamping the cities with job seekers in need of employment and to reduce urban unemployment, the party-state revived the ancient **hukou (household registration)** system in the late 1950s. The *hukou* system was aimed to enforce a strict control over all migration from rural to urban areas, as well as to impose severe limits on the job mobility of workers. In addition, managers of individual state enterprises and construction projects were not allowed to hire workers directly. Instead, workers were recruited by state labor bureaus and then allocated to state enterprises in accordance with the priorities set by the central state planners.

Third, the Chinese working class was a product of the Maoist socialist revolution. In the 1950s, the party-state's socialist objectives were unmistakable. Since Marx had proclaimed that socialism would reunite labor with means of production, the Maoist party-state had set up a modern industrial system based on the principals of (1) permanent job tenure and (2) working provision of a wide range of welfare benefits.

The Chinese **work unit** (*danwei*) model was at the extreme in terms of the fixed nature of employment. Core workers were given an implicit collective guarantee not only of jobs for life, but also jobs for life for their descendents. Although Chinese workers were paid wages, labor power was not seen as a commodity because there was no real labor market. There was always a surplus of labor, but the movement of individuals was strictly controlled through *hukou* (household registration), food rationing, and labor assignment policies. Rural residents were members of their village production brigades, urban residents were members of their work units, and there was little movement among them.

As Andreas (2012) points out, while it is true that Chinese workers did not own the factories in which they worked (the factories which were all public property managed by the state), workers did, however, own their jobs. They were lifetime members of their work units. They enjoyed the provision of full sick leave, maternity, retirement, medical, and injury benefits. Many of these benefits extended to family members as well.

In capitalism, the responsibility for the overall social reproduction of the working class is left to the state — which through the provision of a system of universal welfare ensures that workers are able to sustain themselves through periods of unemployment, ill health, while the education and training of a new generation of workers ensures that workers are fit and healthy at work. In contrast, in Maoist China where the party-state had become fused with capital, the *danwei* (work unit) system was designed to ensure that much of the welfare functions of the state became devolved to each individual state enterprise. Thus, Chinese workers would eat in the company canteens, live in the company-provided flats, and go to the company doctors. Walder (1984) points out the *danwei* (work units) were often able to provide a very broad array of worker needs, such as rations and foodstuffs, meal halls, subsidized food, housing medical care, factory clinics and hospitals, kindergartens, nurseries, primary schools, vocational schools, and other resources.

The *danwei* not only reproduced the workforce as a community, it also politically integrated the workers into the party-state. The party cell set up in each *danwei* was the basic party unit in both industry and the urban areas. As such, *danwei* served to mediate between the state bureaucracy and the working class. The party cells served as the means to mobilize the workers behind the objectives of the party (Aufheben, 2008). Raymond Lau (1997) points out that the enterprise party committee operated a security department, which was simultaneously an arm of the public security bureau. Lifelong employment in state enterprises serving as mini-"welfare states" made workers totally dependent on them. Dossiers were maintained on each and every individual worker, in which any sign of dissatisfaction was recorded (Walder, 1986).

INEQUALITY AND CONFLICT IN THE *DANWEI*

Although the Maoist party-state had advocated the ideology of egalitarianism, the *danwei* work unit still gave rise to a class hierarchy with its own peculiar characteristics. To start with, there was a distinct hierarchy of work units, where the largest units run by central ministries — especially those in priority industries such as steel and machinery — were much better endowed than smaller units run by local authorities. At the bottom of urban hierarchy, there were small collective enterprises created by street committees or parent factories, largely for the purpose of employing housewives and young people for whom the party-state had not provided jobs in state-owned units. Indeed, although all workplaces were supposed to have their own *danwei,* it was only in the larger and high-ranking industries that the *danwei* were fully developed.

Moreover, workers in *danwei* were further subdivided according to their work status, i.e., whether they are classified by permanent workers versus temporary workers. Temporary workers could take form of seasonal workers, casual workers, or contracted workers (Walder, 1984). State enterprises occasionally have short-term labor needs that exceed their planned labor allocation. Sometimes a state industrial enterprise contracted with a construction team is made up of rural workers to complete a project — usually construction, excavation, or moving and hauling. However, temporary workers are not eligible for any of the fringe benefits that permanent state workers normally receive and they are officially denied the opportunity to become permanent state employees when they complete their contracts.

As a whole, the Chinese working class under Maoism had made great strides in wages, welfare, employment security, and social status. The Chinese workers could enjoy stable, secure income; socially provided housing, medical care and children education; guaranteed lifetime employment; a work environment that often involved considerable workers' power, and social and political prestige. Starting in the 1950s, Chinese workers benefited from a way of life and a standard of living to be envied even by the workers in the advanced European countries (Blecher, 2002).

It must be pointed out that employment security and welfare were the fruits of class struggle, i.e., only after the West European workers formed a class and their labor unions engaged in intensive struggles for over a century that they could secure enough concessions from the capitalist class to attain a fairly decent living standard. However, the Chinese working class was simply awarded employment security and welfare gratuitous by the party-state, without going through any class formation and any class struggle with the capitalists.

Since the good fortune of the Chinese working class depended solely on the revolutionary policies of the Maoist party-state, it could easily go astray when the party-state changed its pro-labor policy. When the party-state no longer pursued the Maoist revolutionary agenda in 1978, there were also the rapid remaking of the Maoist working class.

THE REMAKING OF THE MAOIST WORKING CLASS SINCE 1978

The first wave of the economic reforms in the 1980s had unintentionally strengthened both the *danwei* and the Maoist working class. When factory managers were allowed to manage without the day-to-day political interference of the party cells and the party secretaries of the factory, the *danwei* was able to gain a degree of independence *vis-à-vis* the party-state to pursue its own distinct corporate interests. By responding to the party-state's call to increase production, the factory managers re-introduced wage incentives and paying out bonuses to everyone, effectively giving an across-the-board pay rise to their workers. As a result, during the 1980s, *danwei* workers saw improved welfare provision and their wages rose significantly faster than prices. Not only that, with the huge expansion of small-scale consumer-oriented industries bought about by the first wave of reforms, the Chinese working class had access to a far larger range of commodities that they could buy with their higher wages.

Yet, the first wave of reforms was to bring about the following changes that were in the long-run to seriously undermine the *danwei*. First of all, the shift in state investment away from large-scale heavy industries meant that the *danwei* now found itself embedded in declining and increasingly dilapidated industries.

In addition, there was the introduction of **individual labor contracts**. The replacement of the implicit collective guarantees by individual labor contracts was first introduced in the Special Economic Zones in 1984. These labor contract reforms then spread to the rest of China in the late 1980s. By 1989, it was estimated that 95% of all state-run enterprises had introduced labor contracts. These labor contract reforms were made universal with the passing of the new labor contract law in 1994.

Under the labor contract reform, all *existing* workers were given individual life-long employment contracts. However, all workers who were to be subsequently hired were to be given limited-term contracts that provided far less job security. This reform was aimed to reduce employees and increase efficiency. Unfortunately, the reform created crucial generational divisions with the *danwei* between the older generation and the younger generation of workers: while the older workers were still able to keep their lifelong employment, the newly-hired younger workers could only be employed in contract terms. In addition, this reform also meant an end to the hereditary right to a job for the descendents of *danwei* workers. In doing so, the enterprise effectively severed its responsibility for the social reproduction of the *danwei* as a workforce community.

In the early 1990s, it was estimated that as much as a third of urban workforce was surplus to requirements — with much of this superfluous labor concentrated in large-scale heavy industry in the Northeast. Market reformers had long complained that state-owned enterprises were burdened by "multiple objectives" which prevented them from focusing exclusively on maximizing profit. In order to allow them to narrow their focus, they had to be freed from the burdens imposed by a superfluous permanent work force and generous welfare responsibilities. However, the task of making 30 to 40 million workers redundant was certainly a daunting one; particularly as these workers had long served as an important pillar of support of the party-state.

As a result, the party-state had to wait until the late 1990s before it carried out the second phase of the reform which called out mass redundancies in large industries. As more and more state-owned enterprises reached financial autonomy and once the party-state imposed stricter budgetary controls on them, they found themselves with large deficits, mounting debts and recurrent cash flow crises.

Profit and loss now became the overriding concern of factory managers. Not only they had the fear of getting sacked if they failed to turn a profit, with greater financial autonomy they also nurtured hopes of diverting profits into their own pockets. Driven by such hopes and fears, the factory managers were soon to be transformed into efficient "personifications of capital". In the heat produced by such financial pressures and opportunities, any lingering of the paternal ties and community bonds towards the *danwei*, no doubt, soon evaporated; the capitalist factory managers now were eager to dismantle the *danwei* institution by cutting the bloated wage bill and eliminating enterprise welfare with the sole aim to produce a profit.

Thus, when the party-state announced in 1997 that there would be a concerted drive to restructure and rationalize large-scale state-owned enterprises across the whole of China, the "iron rice bowl" of employment guarantees for the Chinese working class was to be finally smashed.

THE THREE GUARANTEES TO DEFUSE WORKING CLASS DISCONTENT

In order to mitigate the impact of the demise of the *danwei* on the tens of millions of workers who were going to lose their jobs, the party-state set up policies which were dubbed as the "three guarantees": Early retirement, Xiagang (off-duty) scheme, and a basic safety net of unemployment benefits.

First, workers in their 40s and 50s, who had been employed before the introduction of individual labor contracts, were to be offered **early retirement** with a pension commensurate with the status of their *danwei.*

Second, workers who were to lose their jobs, but had been employed before labor contracts were introduced in 1986, would not have to severe ties with their former *danwei.* These workers known as **xiagang** (off-duty) are instead on furlough from their old posts. Officially, their old enterprises do not need their services at that time but could re-employ them if they were needed; thus these workers are not officially unemployed. Xiagang workers were still allowed certain fringe benefits like housing, health services. Special re-employment centers were set up to provide transitional support for these workers and were to be funded partly by the state-owned enterprises making the redundancies, partly by the local authorities overseeing the state-owned enterprise in question, and partly by the central government. These re-employment centers would take on the responsibility of paying unemployment benefits and in providing retraining for the xiagang workers for up to three years as well as help these workers to find new employment. After three years are over, the re-employment centers can terminate their relationship with the workers, and with the worker's relationship to their *danwei*. This xiagang "off-duty" scheme was aimed to cushion the shock of unemployment and the class antagonism of state workers against the state.

Finally, municipal governments were to provide a **basic safety net of unemployment benefits** for all urban workers that had been made redundant. That was to ensure financial support for those laid-off workers too young to qualify as xiagang, as well as those xiagang workers who were still unemployed after three years.

Despite the above guarantees to protect the laid-off workers, there are still several structural problems caused by the economic restructuring. First of all, the responsibility of implementing these "three guarantees" were left to the initiative of factory managers and lower- and middle-ranking officials in the local governments, who often had their own priorities for the limited amounts of funds at their disposal. For the factory managers, they would prefer to use the funds to pay off the debts of their state-owned enterprise, so they could borrow more from the banks in order to meet the cost of restructuring (like new investment in new plant and machinery). Factory managers would see the fund as being wasted if it went to paying laid-off workers to do nothing. Likewise, local authorities are eager to invest in infrastructure (like road and electricity) in order to attract foreign capital to their areas rather than to divert money earmarked for funding the "three guarantees". In addition, the more unscrupulous factory managers and local party-state officials were often in a position to divert the "three guarantees" funding from the central government into their pockets.

Too often, payments to pensioners and xiagang workers were seriously delayed, paid intermittently, or were far less than were due. At the same time, local governments used whatever excuse they could find to disqualify laid-off workers from claiming the basic unemployment benefits. As a result, the implementation of the "three guarantees" fell far short of the promises made by the party-state leadership. Millions of laid-off workers and pensioners plunged into poverty and were obliged to supplement whatever welfare benefits their family could extract by becoming street vendors or undertaking whatever causal employment they could find (Lee, 2007).

As the following sections discuss, it was the contradiction between the promises made by the central party-state leadership and their actual implementation by what is regarded as the corrupted local state authorities and factory managers that was to form the matrix within which the struggle of the Maoist working class has developed.

STRUGGLES OF THE MAOIST WORKING CLASS

The Chinese working class has responded to the above reform policies by a new wave of labor protests. Tim Pringle (2002, p. 1) reports that "almost every week in Hong Kong and mainland China, newspapers bring reports of some kind of labor action: a demonstration demanding pensions; a railway line being blocked by angry, unpaid workers; or collective legal action against illegal employer behavior such as body searches or forced overtime".

According to the official statistics, in 1998, there were 6,767 collective actions (usually strikes or go-slows with a minimum of three people taking part) involving 251,268 people. This represented an increase in collective actions of 900% from 1990s. In 2000, this figure further jumped to 8,247 collective actions involving 259,445 workers (Pringle, 2002, p. 2). Given such widespread labor protests, no wonder that the Chinese government has identified labor problem as the biggest threat to China's social and political stability (Chen, 2000; Lee, 2000).

The following cases reported by Feng Chen (Chen, 2000) aptly illustrate the pattern of labor protests:

- On August 8, 1994, more than 300 miners in a molybdenum mine at Yangjiazhangzi, Liaoning province, protested against wage arrears by blocking the local highway.
- On April 13, 1998, about 200 retired workers from a large plant in Wuhan city sat at an intersection of a main street and displayed

banners that demanded the payment of their pensions, which had been delayed over six months.

- In March 1999, 500 laid-off coal miners demonstrated in front of the city government headquarters in Chengdu, the capital of Sichuan province, after being unpaid for three months. They displayed banners asking for food. The protest lasted for three days.

However, it must be pointed out that the above growing incidence of labor protests has not led to the rise of labor movement. In general, the labor protest in post-socialist China bears the following characteristics (So, 2007, p. 135):

- *Short duration*: less than 10 days;
- *Small size*: less than 500 people;
- *Compartmentalized*: the protests are isolated from one another, without spreading from one region/industry to another;
- *Economistic*: mostly bread-and-butter issues, seldom raises political issues or structural issues; and
- *Legalistic*: mostly petitions that go through the existing legal laws and procedures with an appeal to local authorities, and stay within legal limits.

In short, labor protest in China tends to be "spontaneous, small-scale, short-lived, compartmentalized, economistic, and stayed within legal bounds". In the literature, labor protests are also characterized as "short-lived, economically motivated episodes", "spasmodic, spontaneous and uncoordinated", and "spontaneous, leaderless" (Lee, 2000, p. 50; Blecher, 2002, p. 285; Chen, 2000, p. 62). Obviously, these small-scale, short-lived, spontaneous labor protests have failed to generate a national labor movement.

As such, an important research question to be asked is: Why there is no labor movement in post-socialist China? Despite economic reforms intensifying the structural contradictions against the Chinese workers, and despite widespread labor protests since the 1990s, why did they fail to generate significant strike waves and protest movements all over China? In other words, despite the Chinese workers' participation in labor protests and class struggles, why did they fail to form a class to protect their class interests?

This chapter argues that the communist party-state has played a decisive role in the shaping of the contour of labor protests in post-socialist China. To highlight the decisive role played by the party-state, the following section will examine how the party-state carried out policies to create social divisions within the working class, to impose political repression to disorganize the working class, to set up labor legislations to pre-empt labor protests, to adopt the tactics of accommodation to diffuse labor protests, and to maintain a moral high ground by shifting the blame to lower-level officials. Finally, this chapter will examine the future of labor protests and discuss its implication for the China's development.

Create Social Divisions Within the Working Class

In the Maoist era, there was little significant division among the Chinese workers employed in the state sector. In general, all state workers enjoy stable, secure income, socially provided housing, health care and education, and guaranteed lifetime employment. However, in the reform era, there were several state policies that resulted in creating deep social division in the working class.

First, there is the division between the employed and the unemployed workers. In order to ease the pain of unemployment for state workers, the state adopted a policy called "off-duty" (*xiagang*). "Off-duty" workers were those who still maintained "employment relations" with the state enterprises, potentially re-employable if business improves, and who received livelihood allowances amounting to only a tiny fraction of regular income. Cai Yongshun points out that labor protests were mostly carried out by laid-off workers in the state-owned enterprises, while the employed workers and xia-gang workers seldom offered any support (Cai, 2002, pp. 327–344).

Second, there is the division between urban workers and migrant workers. Through the *hukou* household registration system, the party-state allowed the peasants to leave their farms but not their villages. Thus, the peasants are allowed to work in market towns and urban cities only as temporary migrant workers. They have no right to settle down permanently in these territories. As will be discussed in more detail in the next chapter, a new class of temporary migrant workers, many of them young women known as *dagong mei* (maiden workers), have emerged in response to the employment opportunities in the export-processing zone in the Southern provinces. An estimated 100 million temporary migrant workers have left the countryside to enter towns and cities in search of non-agricultural jobs in the 1990s. This *hukou* household registration system has created a *segmented labor market*. Urbanites work as permanent workers in the state sector or in high-paying primary labor markets which provided health care and other benefits. On the other hand, rural temporary migrants could only get jobs in the secondary labor market in the private and collective sectors, and pick up jobs that pay low salary and provide few benefits.

Such labor market conditions have led to a divided working class. This class division was reinforced by residential segregation and ethnic stereotyping. Temporary migrant workers tend to live in very poor quality housing in the urban fringe. Migrant housing generally lacks facilities such as electricity, water supply, drainage and sewage systems, and fire prevention lanes. In addition, temporary migrant workers are regarded as outsiders and excluded from the local society. Local urban workers have assigned many negative ethnic labels to migrant enclaves, including "paradise of thieves and robbers", "camps for prostitutes", "retreats of hunted criminals", etc. Tensions have been growing between urban workers and temporary migrant workers (Taubmann, 2000).

As Lee (2000, p. 58) points out, "local urban workers and migrant workers are not ready allies in forming any class-based movement. Divided by localistic origins (local workers versus outside workers), sociocultural backgrounds (country folk versus urbanites), and age (young versus middle-aged and older), the two groups of workers often find themselves in competition for the same unskilled and low-paid manufacturing jobs in both the state and the non-state sectors. ... Even when they labor side by side within state-owned factories, conflicts regarding wage rates and work allocations are common".

Impose Political Repression to Disorganize the Working Class

In order for the working class to form a class, it needs its own organization and its own leaders to concentrate its resources, to disseminate information, to articulate its interests and discourse, to plan strategy and tactics, etc. However, a fundamental problem for the Chinese working class is that they are disorganized, and their protests are often leaderless. Why is that so? What explains the lack of its own class organization and leaders for the Chinese working class?

First of all, although enterprises were supposedly to form labor unions to protect the interests of workers, but unions formed in foreign-invested enterprises were mostly "company unions", i.e., they were led and staffed by management personnel who were mainly responsible for collecting union fees, organizing birthday parties and recreational events. These union leaders were also salaried shop floor supervisors or section heads in the factory administration (Lee, 2000, p. 51). Thus, they were on the side of management rather than on the side of workers when labor conflict broke out.

Similarly, although the All-China Federation of Trade Unions (ACFTU) are supposedly to take care of the interests of the workers in state-owned enterprises, Lee Ching Kwan (2000, p. 55) reports that the ACFTU has proved to be too weak to protect workers rights. In fact, there is widespread disillusion among rank-and-file workers towards the ACFTU, as most workers turn not to the ACFTU but to informal networks for support when their rights are encroached upon. More often than not, official unions are controlled directly by management. Indeed, many studies demonstrate that the AFCTU routinely act on behalf of the party-state and management and some scholars consider the official unions are simply state organs (Taylor and Li, 2007) or part of the government bureaucracy (Friedman,

2009) that pursues the interests of the party-state and the employers, rather than the interests of the workers.

In 1989, taking advantage of the rebellious climate in the Tiananmen Square, Beijing workers attempted to form a Beijing Workers' Autonomous Federation (BWAF). This attempt greatly frightened the communist party leaders, as BWAF had the potential for the workers to form an alliance with intellectual and human rights dissidents. Subsequently, BWAF met with ruthless suppression by the party-state.

In November 1999, the government announced new rules for public gatherings, requiring assemblies larger than 200 to obtain approval from local public security authorities. Gatherings, larger than 3,000, would require the approval of security offices from a higher level. Since then, the communist party leaders continue to arrest, convict, and imprison any labor activists who try to form an independent labor organization and start a violent protest, and just to make their intentions clear the party leaders "ordered cities across the country to augment their anti-riot police" in January 2001 (Eckholm, 2001).

Under this repressive environment, Cai (2002) reports that workers in labor protests tend not to resort to violent or dramatic forms of action because such actions would increase the hostility around such protests and would invite the suppression by the party-state. Such repressive environment also leads to a pattern of *leaderless protest* because being an organizer does not bring a person more benefits but puts the person in a risky situation because of state repression. If individuals anticipate a risk of violence, they may refuse to assume a leadership role. As some labor activists admit: "We only work as consultants, because organizing is too sensitive. ... We research the workers' situation; find out what ways work best. We only help workers who requests help. If they do not request help it is best to keep a distance from them" (Cai, 2002, pp. 336–337).

Without organization and leadership, it is difficult to wage large-scale protests over a long period of time. As a result, Chinese labor protests tend to be small-scale, unplanned (spontaneous), and short-lived.

Set Up Labor Legislations to Pre-empt Labor Protests

In addition to bolstering its coercive means of repression, the Chinese state also tried to institutionalize labor conflict through setting up a national labor dispute arbitration system. By 1997, some 270,000 labor dispute mediation committees at the enterprise level, and 3,159 labor dispute arbitration committees at county, city and provincial levels were established. These committees have been constituted by a "tripartite principle" and have representatives from the state, labor, and the employer. In the last decade, enterprise mediation cases amounted to 820,000, while 450,000 cases of labor arbitration were processed (Lee, 2000, p. 47). The national hierarchy of labor dispute arbitration mechanism attests to the state's attempt to provide institutional channels for the resolution of labor conflicts during economic reforms. The emphasis is on pre-emption and mediation at the enterprise level, with arbitration at the local committee level. Submission of labor disputes to the civil court is the last resort.

In 2007, the party-state passed three new labor laws to strengthen the administrative absorption of labor struggles (Leung and So, 2013; Hui and Chan, 2011, pp. 164–165). These three new laws are: The Employment Promotion Law, the Labor Dispute Mediation and Arbitration Law, and the Labor Contract Law. The Employment Promotion Law aims to provide guidelines to local government on how to monitor employment agencies, as well as facilitate occupational training for workers. The Labor Dispute Mediation and Arbitration Law simplifies the legal procedure of mediation and arbitration, reducing the money and time costs to workers using these procedures. The Labor Contract Law, which is regarded as the single most important of the three new laws, seeks to stabilize employment relations by making it the legal obligation of employers to sign formal labor contracts with workers. Moreover, the Labor Contract Law clearly states under what conditions, and with what procedures, employers can legally terminate a labor contract and their penalties if they fail to do so (So, 2010a).

As a result, Chinese workers have seized this institutional space to redress grievances and defend their rights. Most of their disputes are economic in nature, with wages, welfare and social insurance payments being the most common causes of conflicts. Wage arrears are particularly pronounced in private and foreign-invested firms.

Thus, most workers have tried the labor dispute system first to express their grievances; only when they fail to get what they want, they engage in labor protests publicly. In this respect, the national dispute system has pre-empted workers from engaging in labor protest and public demonstrations. Had the labor dispute system not instilled in the 1990s, labor protests would be more widespread and the possibility of it growing into a massive labor movement more likely.

Adopt the Tactics of Accommodation to Diffuse Working Class Protest

Although the party-state made it clear that it is determined to suppress any labor protest organized by independent unions, turned violent, or politically oriented, the state was also quite willing to accommodate the requests of the labor protests if they are economistic, if they do not engage in any violent behavior, or if they stay within legal bounds. This accommodation policy of the state had greatly influenced the nature of labor protests emerged in the last decade: Labor protests were narrowly confined to be the type that is tolerated by the state and they have a chance to win some concessions.

Chen (2000, pp. 41–63) reports that most of the labor protests by the state workers could be labeled as "subsistence struggles". It was when the workers were plunged into a subsistence crisis, as their wages went unpaid for months, their medical reimbursements were denied and jobs disappeared, that they participated in protests. These workers did not demand to have their previous economic status back, but rather shouted slogans and displaced banners that declared the following:

- "We Want Jobs";
- "We Want Food";

- "We do not Demand Fish or Meat, Just Some Porridge";
- "Not a Yuan in Six Months, We Want Rice to Eat"; and
- "We Need to Eat, We Need to Survive".

These slogans and banners conveyed the desperation and outrage of the retired or unemployed workers, and also showed that their claims focused on demands for subsistence.

The government generally adopted a policy of conciliation and emphasized the use of "persuasion" and "education" to resolve the conflicts. Unless the protests turned into riots, local authorities usually dispersed workers not by force but by promises to redress their concern about their subsistence. On the other hand, since this kind of "subsistence struggles" had only local, economistic demands (such as the need of emergency relief fund, or postponing and revising plant closure or relocation decisions), they were not that difficult to meet. A temporary stop-gap measure by the local state officials was usually what was needed to silence the labor protest.

The willingness of the state to accommodate the demand of "subsistence struggle" explains why the labor protests were usually short-lived, confined to local areas, and failed to escalate into a large-scale social movement that involved workers from other areas or other industries.

Maintain a Moral High Ground by Shifting the Blames to the Lower-Level Officials

In China's labor protest, local enterprises managers and local government officials, not central government officials, were often the target of attack. In fact, the higher-level government officials often punished the local officials (or overturned the lower-level officials' decision) in order to silence the disgruntled workers.

As a result, despite of widespread labor protests, the party-state was able to maintain moral grounds and was immune from the attack of workers. Corruption and poor management decisions were located at the individual level, instead of at the structural level. It was the local officials and enterprise managers who were corrupted and took bad decisions that threatened the subsistence level of the workers. The higher-level officials in the central state had made it very clear that they would not tolerate the mistakes committed by lower-level officials. The central state and the higher-level officials claimed that they and their economic reforms had done nothing wrong to cause the falling living standard and poverty of the workers.

In post-socialist China, Marc J. Blecher reports that since workers generally accepted the hegemony of the state and of the economic reforms, they blamed their enterprise managers (rather than the state or the new economic system) for their bad luck and poverty. A worker had the following to say during Blecher's interview:

"Yes, of course it is unfair that my wages are lower and I have to endure wage arrears just because I happen to work in a plant that is not doing well. Does the state have responsibility? The state's policies are good. It is the implementation that is not good. Sometimes middle-level officials mess things up… Some people just turn bad after becoming officials." (Blecher, 2002, p. 291)

By accepting the discourse that it was the local- or the middle-level officials who were at fault, the Chinese workers appealed to the Central government to solve the problem of corruption or bad management in local government and local enterprises. By taking the moral high ground of the central government for granted, the workers thus wanted to seek help from the central state rather than to challenge its legitimacy. In this respect, labor protests could at most lead to the firing of some local or middle-level officials, but could not result in the development of a highly conscious working class who want to transform the existing economic system.

RAPID ECONOMIC DEVELOPMENT AND MARKET HEGEMONY

The state's policies to divide and de-mobilize the workers were greatly assisted by the rapid economic development of China over the past three decades, which recorded an amazing growth rate of

10% per year. A booming economy is not conducive to labor movement for the following reasons.

A booming economy would provide more resources for the state and the capitalists to grant concessions to the workers to satisfy their "subsistence struggles". In addition, a booming economy would also divert away from politics the energies of lively, smart people with leadership potential. In Cai's (2002) study, the leaders who emerged in the spontaneous labor protest were mostly elite workers who had good social networks. These kind of elite workers were likely to find employment elsewhere in a booming economy, thus they would not put a risk on their careers by participation in labor protests.

Furthermore, a booming economy would lend further support to the market hegemony, i.e., the economic reforms were good and there could be no return to the Maoist period; if the worker was not doing well, it was due either to bad luck or to lousy enterprise managers. The worker should try to think of a better way to make more money in the booming economy rather than participate in labor protests.

In sum, a booming economy lends support to the ideology of market; it is not conducive to promote a national labor movement that aims to achieve systemic transformation.

THE FUTURE OF LABOR INSURGENCY IN CHINA

In this chapter, I argue that economic reforms have done great harm to the Chinese working class in terms of job security, wages, and entitlements (such as housing, health care, and education). Subsequently, the Chinese working class responded by engaging in protests, and the number of labor protests have significantly increased over the past two decades. However, all these massive labor protests have failed to produce a nation-wide labor movement. The aim of this chapter is to show that the state has played a decisive role in shaping the contour of labor insurgency in China.

The state has created deep social divisions in the working class, has prevented the working class forming its own organization, has set up labor legislations to pre-empt labor protests, has pushed the protest towards the direction of "subsistence struggles", and has punished middle-level officials in order to maintain a moral ground. In addition, a booming economy has greatly facilitated the state to impose an ideological hegemony over the workers, making the workers to blame themselves rather than making claims on systemic change.

If the suppression, the diffusion, and the containment of labor insurgency by the state are so successful, what is the prospect for labor insurgency in China? Does the labor movement have any future in China? Given the fact that labor insurgency is a product of the structural contradictions of the economic reforms, labor insurgency could never be completely eliminated if the economic reforms are continued. Like an active volcano, labor protests could be intensified and exploded when the following two facilitating conditions are present.

First of all, labor insurgency could be intensified if there is a downturn in the economy, leading to massive unemployment. If an economic boom like the present helps the state to contain and diffuse the labor protests, then an economic recession in the future may help to intensify the labor protests into a large-scale labor movement. During an economic downturn, not only labor protest would gain more support from the workers, but the state would be deprived of the vital resource to make concessions to protest workers.

In addition, labor insurgency could be intensified if there is a political crisis created by elite cleavages. Changes in ruling alignments create an opportunity structure for the growth of the labor protests and the expansion of social movements. As Andrew Walder (1997, pp. 344–345) points out, "Tiananmen is a classic case in which nascent protests interact with a divided elite and party-state apparatus … with impulses for protests from below". If there is another elite division and power struggle during the regime transition, it is possible that labor protests — in conjuncture with democracy movements and other social movements — could be powerful enough to challenge the party-state's monopoly of power.

In short, although labor insurgency is at present confined to economistic, localized, and peaceful resistance, it does have the potential of becoming a revolutionary movement if the conditions of economic downfall and political crisis are present.

Chapter 6

THE MAKING OF THE NEW MIGRANT WORKING CLASS IN SOUTH CHINA*

In *Against the Law*, Ching Kwan Lee (2007) points out that the migrant working class in South China has followed a different trajectory from that of the veteran state workers in the North in terms of its grievances, actions taken, subjective identity and pattern of mobilization. Working mostly in private, joint-ventures and foreign enterprises in South China, the 100,000,000-strong migrant workers account for around 60% of China's industrial workforce. In the garment and textile industries, these migrant workers constitute 70–80% of the total workforce (Lee, 2007, p. 6). Since the 1990s, these young migrant workers have engaged in protests and strikes (or what the Chinese authorities vaguely refer to as "spontaneous incidents").

In terms of *grievances*, the overwhelming majority of the conflicts for migrant workers in South China are about wages (such as unpaid wages, illegal wage deductions, substandard wage rates, or lack of injury compensation) and working conditions (extremely long working hours, arbitrary and unreasonable factory discipline). In contrast, the conflicts for state workers in North China are about collective consumption (such as housing, pensions, health care and other goods/services in the working class community that were previously given to the workers who had been laid off). An official

---

*This chapter is an updated version of an earlier paper co-authored by Parry Leung and Alvin Y. So (Leung and So, 2012). I want to thank Parry Leung for his permission to include the co-authored paper in this volume.

survey in 2003 showed that about 75% of migrant workers had experienced wage nonpayment over varying periods of time and for varying amounts (Kuhn, 2004, p. 30).

In terms of *actions taken*, migrant workers resort first to legal activism, such as filing petitions and lawsuits for collective labor arbitration, mediation and litigation. Many cases of labor disputes are characterized by migrant workers' self-consciously law-abiding principles of action. They stake their claims in the law, clamoring against violation of labor rights by employers and discrimination against them as "outsiders" or second-class citizens by local state officials. Only when the legal and bureaucratic channels fail (which they often do), migrant workers resort to direct action in the form of slowdowns, collective quitting, strikes, walkouts and other forms of public demonstration.

In terms of *subjective identity*, migrant workers have a muted class consciousness, for they rarely speak of themselves as the "working class" (*gonggrenjieji*) and "workers" (*gongren*) even though some of them have worked in urban factories for more than a decade. Instead, migrant workers still typically identify themselves as peasants (*nongmin*), a place-based status marked by their household registration that defines their legal status. Many also identify themselves as "non-state workers" (*mingong*), "peasant workers" (*nongmingong*) or "outside workers" (*wailaigong*). Lacking in urban household registration and working outside the state sector, migrant workers in South China do not see themselves as real workers, much less as the politically and ideologically privileged "working class" in Maoist socialism.

Finally, in terms of patterns of *mobilization*, migrant workers' labor resistance can be characterized as "cellular" activism, which has been bottled up at either the enterprise or the workshop level and seldom evolves into lateral, cross-locality rebellion. The migrant workers' political targets have remained the local government and the local companies rather than higher-level officials or the Central Government. This localized and fragmented mode of labor mobilization seldom demonstrates a tendency to become radicalized and politicized. Lee (2007, pp. 22–23) explains that the availability of land use rights in their birth villages and the subsistence economy they support act as a safety valve for migrant workers' city survival and dampens migrant workers' resilience in sustained labor struggles.

From a class perspective, Ching Kwan Lee's study (2007) presents a very depressing picture of the making of the migrant working class (MWC) in South China. Lee's work suggests that the MWC is powerless to defend its own interests. It is absorbed in taking *individual* action about personal gains and losses, but has seldom taken any *collective* action; that is, it has not taken any action to improve the working conditions of the entire working class in South China. In addition, the MWC is mostly focused on narrow *economic* issues (such as wage nonpayment) and it generally fails to raise any *political* issues (such as challenging arbitrary factory discipline) in the factories. Although the MWC occasionally rises up in protest, its action tends to be directed through existing legal channels, thus it takes the existing institutions for granted rather than challenging their legitimacy. Although the MWC experiences brutal exploitation at work, it has a *muted class consciousness* and identifies itself as peasant rather than as worker. In summary, the MWC has not yet formed a "class" in a Marxist sense, and the MWC is a merely a class in itself, but not a class for itself. As such, an interesting research question is: under what conditions could migrant workers in South China become a "class" to protect their interests and become an agency in historical transformation?

Since class is not a structure but a set of dynamic processes of perpetual re-creation and constant change of form and composition (Wallerstein, 1979), we need to trace the historical evolution of the MWC in order to say anything about its class potential and trajectory. In retrospect, the second half of the first decade of the 21st century (that is, 2005–2010) seems to have provided a golden opportunity for the formation of the migrant working class in South China.

HISTORICAL DEVELOPMENT IN THE FIRST DECADE OF THE 21ST CENTURY

Ching Kwan Lee's study (2007) was mostly about the profound post-socialist transformations during the last two decades of the 20th century. Thus, it may not be able to capture the four significant historical developments in the first decade of the 21st century, namely, the formation of a second generation of migrant workers, the passing of the new Labor Contract Law by the National People's Congress in June 2007, the global economic crisis since late 2008 and the waves of strikes and labor actions including the Honda strike and workers' suicides at Foxconn in 2010.

The first historical development was the formation of a new generation of Chinese migrant workers (Chan and Pun, 2010). In June, 2010, the All China Federation of Trade Unions (ACFTU) reported that "the post-80s generation" migrant workers were quite different from their parents and the older migrant workers with regard to their childhood experience, their social identity and their demands for decent working conditions (ACFTU, 2010).

The new generation could be labeled as the "second generation" because some of them were raised in urban settings, having followed their migrant families during childhood, or were raised in villages while one or both parents worked in the cities. In fact, the great majority were "left-behind children", as their parents were migrant workers working far away during their childhood; these "left-behind children" find migrant work a natural (if not the only) choice as the great majority cannot get university admission. They leave their villages or towns immediately after finishing school to seek urban jobs. Waged employment in large towns and cities has become the primary means of making a living for these young migrants. The second generation migrant workers have either never farmed the piece of land allocated to them (about 0.07 hectares per person), or have recognized that it is too small to make a living. Moreover, as this land is nontransferable, many migrant workers choose to lease it (under their name) to their neighbors free of charge, which means that they could not possibly return to their villages if they became unemployed in the cities.

Perhaps reflecting this change of childhood experience among the second generation, the ACFTU reported that there has been a transformation of social identity for migrant workers. The second generation identifies itself equally as "peasants" (32.3%) and "workers" (32.3%), whereas the first generation identifies itself more as "peasants" (54.8%) than as "workers" (22%).

The second generation is also more educated and increasingly aware of its rights; second-generation migrants have higher expectations of getting fair work opportunities, and labor and social welfare services. Furthermore, they are demanding greater equality and they have higher aspirations for career advancement than their older counterparts (Chan, 2013).

The second historical development that has helped in shaping an MWC is the passing of the Labor Contract Law by the National People's Congress in June 2007. The new Labor Contract Law is aimed to protect workers' legitimate rights to wages, benefits, welfare and employment security. Many scholars have called the Labor Contract Law the most significant piece of Chinese labor legislation in more than a decade (Chan, 2009; Wang *et al.*, 2009; Becker and Elfstrom, 2010). The Labor Contract Law has the following features:

- *A valid written labor contract* must be offered by the employer before a worker is asked to start working. If an employer has not given a worker a contract after 30 days, a contract is automatically assumed, providing wages and working standards prevalent in the industry in which the worker is employed.
- *Open-ended contracts* for employment are required for those workers who have completed two fixed-term contracts or with more than 10 years of service in a firm. That means a permanent contract of legally valid labor relationship is automatically formed from the date a worker begins to provide substantial labor service to the employer, and workers are protected from dismissal without a valid cause.
- Employers are now obliged to give a *severance payment*, which is about one month for every year the employee has worked in the firm. Previously, employers could offer fixed-term contracts that automatically end without the need for termination or severance pay.

- The new Labor Contract Law also requires employers to *contribute to their employee's social security accounts and set wage standards for workers on probation and overtime* (So, 2010a).

The third historical development shaping the emergence of an MWC is the global economic crisis. The 2008 subprime mortgage crisis in the United States has grown into the deepest economic crisis since the Great Depression. The crisis is no longer simply confined to the financial sector, but has spread to the larger global economy. The 2008 crisis not only marked the end of the golden era of unbridled free-market economics in the United States, but could also serve as a turning point of the capitalist world economy (So, 2012).

At the onset of the economic crisis in late 2008, China's exports suffered a sharp slowdown, down more than 20% from the previous year (Barboza, 2009). In China's Pearl River Delta, many toy export-processing companies have closed or gone bankrupt because of order reductions from the United States and Europe. Roubini (2008) reports that China may be on its way to a hard landing, as the macro-data from China all point toward a sharp deceleration of economic growth, with a sharp fall in spending on consumer durables, falling home sales, and a sharp fall in construction activities. The global economic crisis in 2008 clearly exposes the vulnerability of the Chinese mode of development, which is export-driven and heavily dependent on the subcontracts of transnational corporations.

Unemployment became a growing concern in China's urban areas in late 2008. China needs a growth rate of at least 5% to absorb the 24 million people who join the labor force each year. The sharp decline of export trade has left millions without work and set off a wave of social instability. The *Sunday Times* reported on February 1, 2009 that social unrest among unemployed workers spread more widely in China than was officially reported (Sheridan, 2009).

The fourth historical development in the argument about the emergence of a migrant working class is that 13 young migrant workers attempted or committed suicide at the two Foxconn production facilities in South China between January and May 2010.

Jenny Chan and Ngai Pun (2010, p. 1) "interpret their act as a protest against a global labor regime that is widely practiced in China. Their defiant deaths demand that society reflect upon the costs of a state-promoted development model that sacrifices dignity for corporate profit in the name of corporate growth". The Foxconn case is important because it appeared in the front pages of the global mass media in the spring of 2010. Students and Scholars against Corporate Misbehavior (SACOM), labor unions and rights, groups protested at the Foxconn General Meeting in Hong Kong on June 8, 2010 and declared the day as the Global Day of Remembrance for Foxconn suicide victims. There were protests against Foxconn in San Francisco and in other cities around the world (Chan and Pun, 2010).

In addition, in the summer of 2010, four strike incidents were reported at Honda's production lines in China. The strike at Honda Auto Parts Manufacturing Co Ltd of Foshan, Guangdong started on May 17, 2010. It quickly expanded to 1,900 workers, including permanent full-time workers and vocational school interns. The strike surprisingly lasted for 19 days, until 4 June. In the end, the workers won, getting a 32.4% increase in wages (from RMB 1,544 to RMB 2,044), while the student interns got a 70% increase (from RMB 900 to RMB 1,500).

However, what is significant about the Honda strike is that workers not only raised the demand of forming an independent trade union during the strike, but the strikers were also reported to have had a physical confrontation with official union members on the May 31, 2010. At around 2 pm on 31 May, a Honda worker, who had been interviewed by Chris Chan the day before, sent him a mobile phone message saying that "members from the district trade union started beating strikers in a chaotic situation!" Honda workers later told Chris Chan that the strikers were beaten up by about 200 people mobilized by the town- and district-level trade unions. A few strikers were hurt and sent to a nearby hospital (Chan and Hui, 2012).

Given the above four historical developments in the first decade of the 21st century, what is the recent impact on the making or remaking of the MWC in South China? Before we answer this question, however, we need to point out that class is not a thing or a structure but a set of complex historical relationships with other classes and the state. Thus, a class cannot be studied in isolation from other classes and the state (Thompson, 1978). Therefore, in order to examine the making or remaking of the working class, we need to broaden our scope to examine how the four historical developments in the 21st century have transformed class relations in ways that involve the state, the working class and the capitalist class.

THE REALIGNMENT OF CLASS RELATIONS IN THE 21ST CENTURY

In the 1980s, when China first started to re-enter the capitalist world economy, the Communist Party-state pursued the path of neoliberalism, liberalizing the market, downsizing the state bureaucracy, loosening its regulations, cutting back its social welfare commitments and privatizing its state economy (though not yet embarking on lay-offs in the state sector). However, since the Communist Party-state's survival has been threatened by the growing number of labor protests in the cities and the numerous peasant protests in the countryside at the turn of the 21st century, China has had second thoughts about pursuing the path of neoliberal capitalism in order to pre-empt the further intensification of class conflict (So, 2010b). Under the policy of "building a new socialist countryside" and a "harmonious society", the regime, under the leadership of Hu Jintao and Wen Jiabao, tried to move in a more sustainable direction by balancing economic growth and social development. Not only has the agricultural tax been abolished to help relieve the burden on peasants, but the state has also increased its rural expenditure by 15% (to US$15 billion) to bankroll guaranteed minimum living allowances for peasants, and has funded an 87% hike (to US$4 billion) in the health care budget (Liu and Ansfield, 2007).

Before the arrival of the global economic crisis in 2008, China was already in the process of moving away from the model of neoliberalism. China's strong developmental state enabled it to have a quick response to the global economic crisis. Beijing announced a massive stimulus program in early November 2008 — only seven weeks after the Lehman Brothers' collapse. China's stimulus package was budgeted at RMB 4 trillion (US$586 billion), which was equivalent to 13.3% of China's 2008 GDP. It is one of the largest economic stimulus packages (both in spending levels and as a percentage of GDP) that have been announced by the world's major economies to date (Morrison, 2009, p. 6).

Aside from promoting capital accumulation, the stimulus program aimed to soften the acute class conflict that emerged as a result of rapid development over the past three decades. For example, in 2009, the state announced plans to spend an additional US$124 billion over the next three years to create a universal health care system. The health plan would attempt to extend basic coverage to most of the population by 2011, and would invest in public hospitals and training for village and community doctors. Efforts have also been made to boost rural incomes and spending levels and narrow the gap in living standards between rural and urban citizens. For example, since February 2009, an estimated 900 million Chinese rural residents have been eligible to receive a 13% rebate for the purchase of home appliances; in addition, public housing, education and infrastructure projects are largely targeted at rural areas (Morrison, 2009, p. 7).

In short, the stimulus program aims to encourage consumer spending in order to boost the domestic economy. The state wants to promote domestic consumption and improve collective consumption and social insurance. The assumption is that unless the social safety net and social insurance are expanded, Chinese consumers will be more inclined to save than to spend, and the enlarged domestic market will not be able to absorb the slack in the export market caused by the global economic crisis of 2008–2009.

Furthermore, the global economic crisis has led to a growing conflict between the Chinese state and the global capitalist class. In August 2009, the Chinese government arrested and prosecuted several executives of a foreign mining giant, the Anglo-Australian company Rio Tinto, accusing them of being spies who had stolen state secrets. Although the spy charges were later dropped, the Rio Tinto executives still faced lesser charges of bribery and theft of trade secrets. These espionage threats caused general unease amongst the transnational companies operating in China, who feared they could face persecution and closed-door trials for engaging in what much of the business world would regard as bare-knuckle business tactics. In late 2010, foreign businesses in China were voicing frustration over China's heavily regulated market — a bureaucratic maze, which many transnational capitalists say is designed deliberately to hamstring non-Chinese players to the advantage of their local competitors. The European Union Chamber of Commerce in China also issued a position paper listing hundreds of market-access problems of foreign companies across a range of industries (Ford, 2010).

Foreign companies have also complained loudly that they are being shut out of the majority of the lucrative government procurement sector. For example, not one of the 25 valuable contracts awarded to companies under the Chinese government's US$586 billion stimulus program went to a foreign-owned company (Jiang, 2010).

If the global economic crisis induced the state to take more aggressive actions to protect Chinese industries from the transnationals, the crisis also induced the state to take a stronger stand to protect the Chinese workers from exploitation in the export sector. The new Labor Contract Law took effect in 2008 despite the transnational business community — as represented by the American Chamber of Commerce in Shanghai, the U.S.–China Business Council and the European Union Chamber of Commerce in China — putting up a strong battle in opposition to the Labor Contract Law (So, 2010a).

In 2010, the Central Committee of the Communist Party and the State Council jointly issued the "No. 1 Central Document", which called for better coordination of rural and urban reforms and highlighted the needs of the new generation of migrant workers (Chan and Pun, 2010, p. 4). These rebalancing efforts across different government levels have had an impact on both rural incomes and migrant wages.

Subsequently, when a series of wildcat strikes broke out against Honda and Toyota in several cities in South and Central China in the summer of 2010, the Central Government allowed the Chinese mass media to cover the strikes in detail. This tacit approval of coverage of the strikes seems to reflect a genuine desire of the Chinese state to see higher wages for the workers so as to increase domestic consumption during the global economic crisis. The above speculation is confirmed by the fact that, soon after the strike wave in the summer of 2010, various local governments in Shenzhen, Nanhai and Beijing quickly announced that they would raise the minimum wage by 10–20% in the following months.

In August 2010, during a high-level Japan–China meeting, Chinese Premier Wen Jiabao further bluntly warned Japan "that its companies operating in China should raise pay for the workers". Wen told the Japanese officials that the cause of labor unrest was the relatively low level of pay at some foreign companies (Browne and Shirouzu 2010).

The Chinese economic miracle is built upon the model of export-led industrialization. Since the turn of the 21st century, China has become the global factory and the workshop of the world. China's exports grew from US\$18.1 billion in 1978 to US\$266 billion in 2001, reflecting an annual growth rate of 12%. By 2001, manufacturing exports accounted for 90% of total exports (Nolan, 2004, p. 910).

In South China, most of the manufacturers are subcontractors or suppliers to such transnational giants as Apple, HP or Nokia, or provide products to Walmart in the global commodity chain. It is well known that profit margins in these subcontractor factories are razor-thin. At the global level, producers from Vietnam, India, Cambodia, Bangladesh and other developing countries are pitted against China in a battle to become suppliers further down the global commodity chain. Thus, the Chinese suppliers are under constant pressure to cut the cost of production so as not to lose out to the lower-level players in the commodity chain.

To survive in this brutal and cut-throat market, Chinese manufacturers rely upon what Ching Kwan Lee (2007, p. 162) calls "localistic despotism". In South China, thanks to the patron–client relationship between foreign investors and local officials, the local state seldom intervenes in the factory to regulate labor relations. Thus, the capitalists are free to do whatever they want in order to extract the labor power they purchased; they operate the factory like a "satanic mill", which runs at such a nerve-racking pace that the physical limits and bodily strength of workers are put to the test on a daily basis. Extreme long hours of work, a highly intensive rate of work and substandard wage rates are common methods that those who subcontract to South China factories use to deal with intensive competition and shrinking profit margins in the global commodity chain.

The contractors of South China factories are highly vulnerable to the increasing regulations imposed by the Chinese state and the fluctuation of orders during the global economic crisis. In the jewelry industry, for instance, the 2008 global financial crisis caused a sudden shrinkage of international demand for luxury jewelry products, which resulted in the sudden drop of overseas orders. Also because of the credit crisis, foreign buyers delayed paying their bills, which caused jewelry manufacturers difficulties in borrowing money from banks to finance their production. Parry Leung's (unpublished) study has found that, during the economic crisis, many jewelry factories carried out the following policies to deal with the new Labor Contract Law and the sudden drop of overseas orders.

First, they put up aggressive *retrenchment policies* to cut labor costs, such as cutting workers' overtime work drastically and requesting that they take leave as long as half a month without pay. Factory expenditure was also cut through wage reduction. Overall, wages in the jewelry industry decreased by around 50% in spring 2009 compared with summer 2008 (before the global financial crisis).

Second, illegal dismissal was also found to be a common practice in jewelry factories during the global economic crisis. The Chinese Labor Contract Law, which took effect on January 1, 2008, guarantees severance payment to workers (which is about one month for every year worked in the factory). In order to lay off workers while avoiding legal severance payments, many jewelry factory subcontractors used various schemes to dismiss workers. One way was to carry out unfair management practices to put workers under tremendous pressure, so workers would be forced to quit "voluntarily". Another way was to adopt harsh and unreasonable factory rules; workers found themselves easily subject to accusations of "serious violation of factory rules", which led to their dismissal without legal compensation. Needless to say, the extensive use of the above unfair dismissal strategies has intensified the labor conflict in the jewelry industry and led to a lot of labor disputes in South China. Individual cases of resentful jewelry workers violently attacking factory management have also been reported.

Finally, jewelry factory subcontractors imposed a stricter factory discipline in order to extract more output or wages from the workers. Golden Manufacture Factory, for example, suddenly imposed an additional set of factory rules in October 2008. Workers were angry because they found the new rules were all related to "wage deductions" by comparing the old rules with the new rules (See Table 6.1).

Since the Labor Contract Law was implemented more or less at the same time as the global economic crisis in 2008, the Law has made it very difficult for the subcontractors of South China factories to survive in a hostile environment of highly fluctuating orders from the transnational companies. The subcontractors' reactions in late 2008 and 2009 — such as retrenchment, unfair dismissals and stricter factory discipline — could be interpreted as the capitalists' desperate methods to hang on to their position in the highly competitive global commodity chain.

However, intensified capitalist control and exploitation and a more pro-worker state during the global economic crisis, coupled with the changing composition of the migrant working class, the new Labor Contract Law and the Honda strike, should provide a golden opportunity for the remaking of the MWC in South China.

Table 6.1:   The old rules and the new rules.

The Old Rules that Took Effect in 2007:

- A total of 15 minutes late is allowed in a particular month. If workers arrive late beyond this limit, 2 yuan per minute shall be deducted from their wage and they will not receive a "Full Attendance Award" for that month.
- No "Full Attendance Award" shall be given to any worker who has arrived late three times or more within a month.
- For those who leave duty earlier than the agreed time, 2 yuan shall be deducted from their wages per minute.
- Standard working hour is 8 hours a day, 26 days a month (a total of 208 hours per month). For workers who fulfill this requirement, a "Full Attendance Award" of 30 yuan will be offered for that month.
- Workers have to stay in their designated workplace during working hours. Those who need to leave to use the toilet or for other matters must get a "Leave Duty Permit" from their supervisor before they leave. Workers who do not observe this requirement will have 50 yuan deducted from their wage each time they commit the offence.
- If a worker is found to be discussing wage information or labor contracts in the workplace, a written warning will be issued to him/her, and a wage deduction of RMB 200 shall be applied afterwards.

Additional Factory Rules that Took Effect in October 2008:

For workers who:

- Change their working position without approval; a wage deduction of RMB 30 shall be applied.
- Sleep during working hour, a wage deduction of RMB 10–50 shall be applied.
- Read newspaper or a book during working hour, a wage deduction of RMB 30 shall be applied.
- Eat food during working hours; a wage deduction of RMB 10–50 shall be applied.
- Slack off or gossip during working hour, a wage deduction of RMB 10–60 shall be applied.
- Do not show up in overtime hour, a wage deduction of RMB 100 or above shall be applied.
- Smoke or read newspaper in the toilet for more than 10 minutes during working hour, a wage deduction of RMB 50 shall be applied.
- Agitate strike or organize worker assembly, or conduct work stoppage on purpose, a wage deduction of RMB 300 and dismissal shall be applied.

(Continued)

Table 6.1:   (Continued)

- Use bad language to insult colleagues, a wage deduction of RMB 100 or above shall be applied.
- Use equipment of other workers without approval, a wage deduction of RMB 50 shall be applied.
- Waste energy, a wage deduction of RMB 50 shall be applied.
- Do not keep their work desk tidy after work; a wage deduction of RMB 20 shall be applied.
- Do not put chair under their desk after work; a wage deduction of RMB 10 shall be applied.

THE REMAKING OF THE WORKING CLASS IN SOUTH CHINA

How has the historical development in the first decade of the 21st century and the realignment of class relations transformed the MWC? We look into three dimensions of the MWC, namely: its consciousness, its action and its pattern of mobilization.

Although the previous generation of migrant workers tended to identify themselves as "peasants" and were focused on the problem of discrimination and had a muted class consciousness, the new generation of migrant workers seems to have shed their peasant identity. These workers are more ready to identify themselves as workers and, in the late 2010s, voiced collective class issues instead of individual discrimination issues. Their class consciousness is heightened when they are in conflict with the capitalist class. For example, many jewelry workers, when they knew that they had been blacklisted by the Jewelry Manufacturer's Association, sent the following message through the internet to enlist support from their fellow workers (Leung, unpublished):

> We were treated unjustly! For those jewelry workers who knew about the secret of the black list, please come forward to help us. We need you to stand in the position of justice and public interest! We need you to speak the truth for workers! At this moment, we need you to join your hands with us to eliminate the jewelry black list and to fight against those black-hearted employers. Solidarity of workers

needed to be achieved. Together we join hands to reveal the dirty secret of the evil-minded trade association in the jewelry industry.

Rising class consciousness can also be seen during the Honda strike in the summer of 2010. On 3 June, workers' representatives issued an open letter to all Honda workers and to the public. At the beginning of the letter it declared (Chan and Hui, 2012):

> We urge the company to start serious negotiation with us and accede to our reasonable requests. The company earns over 1,000 million yuan every year and this is the fruit of our hard work. Honda workers should remain united and be aware of the divisive tactics of the management… *our struggle is not only for the sake of 1,800 workers in Honda, it is also for the wider interest of workers in our country. We want to be an exemplary case of workers safeguarding their rights.*

After the above letter was released on 3 June, workers' representatives received over 5,000 mobile phone messages of support from people all over China. Below are three such support messages (Chan and Hui, 2012):

> You are really on the side of Chinese *workers*. I am furious with what the district and township trade unions have done. *Workers all over the country will support you.*
>
> *You do not only represent Honda workers, but also the 100 million-strong working class under oppression in China…* All the people in the country are supporting you and paying great attention to your action. Your glorious action will be recorded as part of modern Chinese history.
>
> I am a *manual worker* in another Honda factory. Your strike has *set a good example of Chinese workers* furthering their legitimate interests. You are fighting not only for your own interest, but also for the China people. As a manual worker, I fully support you.

Although the previous generation of migrant workers tended to focus on such economic concerns as wage nonpayment, the new generation has raised new *political* claims that challenge the authority of the existing institutions. The Honda strike, for instance, included the democratic reform of the enterprise trade union in their demands on June 3, 2010. Later, they further requested a democratic and formal election of 30 workers' representatives to represent them at the negotiation table.

In response to the demands of the Honda workers, the official Xinhua News Agency commented that it is of great urgency to push forward collective wage consultation in enterprises, so as to further safeguard workers' legal rights and promote harmonious labor relations in China. Kong Xiang Hong, the Vice President of the Guangdong Provincial Federation of Trade Unions (GPFTU), said that he would speed up the democratization of the trade union so his members could elect their own president. Kong also announced a pilot scheme of democratic elections for workplace trade unions and training in 10 factories, including the Honda factory that just had a strike in 2010 (Chan and Hui, 2012; Chan, 2012).

The mobilization capacity of the previous generation of migrant workers was highly limited, as it was confined to a particular enterprise and it could not spread from one workplace to another, from one industry to another, or from one locality to another. However, the constraints of this cellular activism seem to have been broken in 2010, when a wave of strikes spread across factories, across industries and even across regions. Lau and Choi (2010) and Chris Chan (2012) report that the following strikes took place during May and June, 2010 (See Table 6.2).

Overt labor collective resistance did not stop in China following the 2010 strike wave. On the contrary, another wave of labor strikes took place in 2011. In October 2011 alone, at least 10 strikes were reported in Shenzhen, including a strike at the Citizen Watch Factory, a bus driver strike, a teacher's strike and three cab drivers' strikes (Hui and Chan, 2011).

Although the previous generation of migrant workers occasionally rose up in protest, their action tended to be directed through existing legal channels. After years of disappointed legal struggles, however, the new generation of migrant workers seems to be more

Table 6.2:   Strikes between May and June 2010.

Region	Action
Dongguan (Pearl River Delta)	Strike at a shoe factory on June 4, 2010.
Foshan (Pearl River Delta)	Honda workers clash with riot police on May 31, 2010.
Foshan (Pearl River Delta)	250 workers at Guangqi Honda strike on June 7, 2010.
Nansha (Pearl River Delta)	Strike in a Honda factory on June 20, 2010.
Zhongshan (Pearl River Delta)	Strike in a Honda factory on June 25, 2010.
Shenzhen (Pearl River Delta)	Workers at Merry Electronics Co. protest on June 6, 2010.
Huizhou (east of Guangzhou)	2,000 workers of Yacheng Electronic strike on June 7, 2010.
Kunshan (near Shanghai)	2,000 workers at KOK factory clash with riot police on June 7, 2010.
Beijing	Strike in a Hyundai factory on June 23, 2010.
Tianjin	Strikes in two Toyota factories on June 23, 2010.

ready to defend their class interests through strikes or work stoppages rather than through legal disputes and lawsuits. A jewelry worker in South China remarked: "I know the [legal] path would not be easy. I had gone through such painful experiences. It will take years. We will be under big pressure, but we have no choice" (Leung, Unpublished).

In the jewelry industry, workers decided against the legal path at the very beginning. Instead, they found collective actions (such as strikes and work stoppages) more effective for achieving their goal. Only when such collective action failed to work did workers consider the option of litigation.

Many workers know that even when they win their lawsuits against their ex-employers, their ex-employers will make appeals until their cases reach the second court. They then have to wait for another two years or more before the final verdict arrives. Even if the final verdict is in their favor, there is still no guarantee that workers will receive compensation because by then the ex-employers might have fled South China, or their company might have closed down.

Furthermore, workers do not have the financial resources to hire a lawyer, unless they have the connections to seek help from local labor NGOs. Without a lawyer, workers have to represent and defend themselves in court against the professional lawyers of their ex-employers. Making themselves knowledgeable about the legal terms is a very difficult task and presenting those legal terms in court is almost impossible.

Therefore, even though workers might be able to attain a verdict partially favorable to them in the end, they have already paid a high price, not to mention the threats and harassments they might receive during the long legal process. In 2008, after the introduction of the New Labor Contract Law, the environment in which workers pursued these legal struggles became even more difficult, as the total number of labor arbitration cases in 2008 was almost double the 2007 number and so, with the mounting number of cases that needed to be heard, these legal hearings would take years to complete. As they have limited savings with which to support themselves, migrant workers certainly cannot wait that long for the final verdict. Moreover, having seen to the success of the Honda workers, who won a big wage increase after they went on strike in 2010, South China migrant workers must surely feel encouraged to pursue collective actions such as strikes and work stoppages even *before* they go through bureaucratic or legal channels.

In summary, migrant workers in South China seem to be drastically transformed in the first decade of the 21st century. Not only do they identify themselves as workers, but they also use the perspective of class to explain their experiences and sufferings. Their struggles have also moved beyond bread-and-butter economic issues; their mobilizations are no longer trapped by "cellular activism", and they increasingly see the need to go beyond the legal channel to pursue strikes and work stoppages in order to protect their class interests.

Given that, in 2010, migrant workers in South China saw such empowering events as: (1) a wave of strikes that resulted in a dramatic increase in wages; (2) the Honda workers' permission to form an independent and democratically elected trade union following their strike; (3) a large increase in the minimum wage in many

South China cities; and (4) the enforced repayment of back-pay, deposits and unreasonable fines to workers by factory subcontractors after they lost legal disputes, did 2010 signal a turning point in the class formation of the working class in China? Has the migrant working class become empowered to protect its class interests? And, in doing so, has it become an agency to shape the historical development of China?

In conclusion, it seems prudent to say that researchers should not be carried away by the above working class victories of 2010. Although they are indeed promising signs of the rise of the working class in South China, it is simply too early to tell whether class consciousness, independent trade unions, collective action and labor militancy will continue, and will lead to the formation of a conscious migrant working class in South China. Victories in 2010 and 2011 may just be a small first step toward the long march of working class formation. Numerous barriers still have to be overcome, such as the lack of a clear vision, the formation of more independent trade unions and the collusion between local state and factory subcontractors in South China (which makes the local state uninterested in protecting working class interests if it goes against local economic development).

Although it is still too early to tell whether the migrant workers have formed a "class", this chapter has shown that the MWC in South China has been remade and transformed by four historical developments in the first decade of the 21st century. The MWC in South China is no longer passive and no longer takes the existing factory regime of "localistic despotism" for granted, but has tried different means to transform it to a more humane institution. During its struggles for social transformation, the MWC will inevitably transform itself into a more militant, active agency to shape the development of China in the 21st century and beyond.

Chapter 7

THE MAKING AND REMAKING OF THE MAOIST PEASANTRY

THE PEASANT PROBLEM ON THE EVE OF THE SOCIALIST REVOLUTION

In contrast to peasants in medieval Europe, the Chinese peasantry had never been tied to the land by extra-economic feudal dues and obligations. Instead, each peasant household entered into what was primarily economic contractual sharecropping arrangement with the landlord. The peasant household would provide the labor, the landlord would provide the land, and the produce would then be shared in accordance with prior agreement.

Like other densely populated third world nations, the amount of land suitable for cultivation in China was in short supply. A substantial proportion of the Chinese peasantry thus ended up with little or no land. Wen (2001, p. 289) reported that 80% land was controlled by 10% of the population in the countryside — the landlords and the rich peasants. At the other pole, 68% of rural smallholders, tenants, and hired laborers owned a mere 14% land. Land ownership was most heavily concentrated and tenancy rates the highest in the central and southern rice growing areas (Kerkvliet and Selden, 1998, p. 37). Given this vastly unequal distribution of land ownership, the Chinese landlords were in a strong bargaining position and were able to squeeze the peasantry to a large extent.

After handling over a substantial share of his crop to the land-lord and after paying his taxes and dues, there would be very little money left for the Chinese peasant to feed his family, to put aside for hard time, or to pay for necessary extravagances such as weddings and funerals. Without reserve and living close to the margin of subsistence, Chinese peasant household was highly vulnerable to price fluctuations in the commercial agriculture introduced since the 19th century because they had to sell immediately after the harvest when the prices were falling.

The peasant's plight favored the dealer and the speculator, generally in league with the landlord. Dealers had larger reserves, wider sources of information, and better opportunities than the peasant. As the peasants fell into debt after being engaged in commercial agriculture, they had to borrow, often at very high rates. When they could not repay, they had to transfer title of the land to a landlord, leading to the growth of a mass of marginal, landless peasants at the bottom of the social hierarchy in the village (Moore, 1966, p. 219).

China's peasant problem in the early 20th century refers to the rapid expansion of the marginal, landless peasantry. It is this class conflict between landless peasants and landlords which provided the structural base for the Chinese socialist revolution in 1949.

THE MAOIST PEASANTRY DURING THE SOCIALIST REVOLUTION

After coming to power, the communist party-state had brought important changes to the class relations of the Chinese countryside. The national program of land reform started in the late 1940s, and the subsequent program of rapid collectivization of agriculture that took off 10 years later, went a long way towards alleviating the plight of landless peasants.

Land Reform

In China, land reform coincided with civil war and international conflict. Land reform began with programs to reduce rent and interest rates consistent with "United Front" efforts to mobilize all Chinese people against the Japanese invaders. However, Chinese village activists soon pressed ahead with land seizures and redistribution, often in advance of party directives.

William Hinton (1998, p. 148) points out that the massive redistribution of land enabled almost every poor peasant and hired laborers in China to *fanshan* (to turn over), to stand up, to acquire land, often tools, a share in a draft animal, a section or two of house — in other words to acquire the basic means of subsistence, and this egalitarian material base undergirding peasant society remained intact throughout the Maoist socialist era (1949–1976).

In short, land reform equalized land ownership within villages, eliminated tenancy and hired labor, broke the power of the dominant landlord class, and improved the position of small owner–cultivator agriculture. Politically, power in the villages shifted from the landlords and rich peasants (who were stripped of land ownership, humiliated, and sometimes imprisoned and killed) to land reform activists and demobilized soldiers, many of whom from the ranks of the poor peasants. Since land reform was an initiative pressed from above by the communist party-state, it had contributed to the power and the penetration of the state at the village level. Socially, land reform eliminated the major polarized rural social classes rooted in differential land ownership and wealth, producing a striking homogenization and equalization of intra-village incomes and opportunities (Lee and Selden, 2007). Economically, land reform liberated hitherto tightly constrained productive forces, primarily the surplus labor power of the Chinese peasants. By providing returns from land of their own as incentive, land reform led to a rapid increase in production not only on already tilled land but also on newly reclaimed land or newly watered fields (Hinton, 1998, p. 149).

Accelerated Collectivization

Land reform, by redistributing land ownership according to the family size of peasants, also means a thorough privatization of land ownership. This privatization drive, coupled with the reintroduction of market relations into rural China after the end of the civil war, quickly led to class differentiation in the countryside. Larger peasant households, which had many family members and were allocated a larger piece of land in land reform, were getting richer. On the other side, small peasant households, which had elderly parents or young children and were allocated a smaller piece of land in Land Reform, were becoming poorer.

Apart from class differentiation, land reform also led to a fragmentation of land holdings. In Chinese peasant villages, given the small size and scattered distribution of the land holding, the peasant household was only entitled to own an acre or two and plowed 10 strips in many different places. This fragmentation ensured fairness with regard to good and bad, near and far, and steep and level holdings, but it condemned peasants to endless ground breaking with hand-held hoes. It also made mechanization virtually impossible and froze labor productivity at medieval levels (Hinton, 1998, p. 155).

As such, the Chinese communist party-state viewed collectives as the keystone of the socialist transition in the rural areas, even as the Maoist party-state sought to avoid the disasters associated with the Soviet Union's forced collectivization.

In the early 1950s, the party-state had set up small *Mutual Aid Teams* and *Low-Level Cooperatives*. Mutual Aid Teams, which consisted of 20–30 families living in the same village, ensured that the land rights of peasants could remain unchanged. Low-level Cooperatives, which were set up based on pre-existing villages, also allowed the peasants to hold shares of land property.

However, the party-state suddenly accelerated the rate of collectivization and collectivized the entire countryside within one year in 1955–1956. In the *Upper-level Cooperatives* in 1956–1957 and the *People's Commune* in 1957–1958, the natural boundaries of traditional villages were broken; peasants no longer worked with their fellow kins and relatives in the same village, but they had to work and share their harvest with strangers in other villages. In addition, the peasants lost their land rights. The post-1956 collectivization drive reduced villagers' autonomy and their control over land, which passed without compensation to the collectives and tightened the state's control over the rural surplus. Furthermore, collectivization also transferred authority over labor, resources, and the production process from peasant household to cadres and the local party-state. Finally, in 1954–1956, the communist party-state virtually eliminated the market for grain, cotton and vegetables, and initiated a system of compulsory crop sales to the state at low fixed prices.

Great Leap Forward and Retreat from Collectivism

China's Great Leap Forward of 1958–1960 carried collectivism to extremes in order to promote the ideals of revolutionary Maoism. By expanding each collective to a scale of up to 100 villages and mobilizing untapped labor (particularly female labor), the Leap was supposed to move China towards the ideal of communism. Soon, however, the bubble burst as a result of three successive years of bad harvest and China hurtled into a famine that exacted a toll of 15 to 30 million lives (Friedman *et al.*, 1991; Kane, 1988).

The famine prompted a flood of villagers into the cities seeking industrial jobs at the height of the Great Leap. This famine and a sudden influx of rural–urban migration led the communist party-state to impose far-reaching controls over population movement through the institution of *hukou* (household registration) system, dividing city from countryside and binding rural people to their villages in subsequent decades.

In the early 1960s, following the failure of the Great Leap, a three-level system of commune, production brigade, and production team was established as the basis for China's rural collectives for the next two decades. *Communes* were reduced in size to approximately 3,000–3,500 households. As of the mid-1970s, each *production brigade* — a village or cluster of hamlets — averaged 200–250 households, and each *production team* contained some 30–40 households (Oi, 1989).

This three-level collective structure coincided with the resurgence of a limited household economy restricted to private plots and a small window of opportunity in local free markets, as well as the development of rural sidelines and industry.

The Collectivization Experiment and Class Inequality

How should China's collective experiment be evaluated? Hinton (1998) argues that by any objective standard (political, economic, and social), China's land reform and the Maoist collectivization project must be judged as outstanding successes.

Without the underlying egalitarian arrangements set up by the communist party-state, China might follow the periphery path of other third world nations, i.e., having large masses of landless and destitute people to form a huge reserve army of rural proletarians with no reliable sustenance, no place to go, and no place to return to that they call their own.

In China, with the exception of the Great Leap famine years, the communist party-state assured subsistence for its growing rural population. By mobilizing large number of laborers to develop the rural infrastructure, particularly irrigation and soil improvement, and by launching a green revolution on a combination of high-yielding seeds, irrigation and chemical fertilizers, the average annual increase in grain production from 1949 to 1984 (a period that includes the "three bad years" of 1959–1961 when output fell sharply) was 7.42%. This kept grain production well ahead of population growth, which averaged to 2.4% (Hinton, 1998, p. 154).

In addition, the goal of the land reform and collectivization was to break up the exploitation and domination of the parasitic landlord class and replace it with grassroots' communities of equal, small peasant households laboring on their own land and basically running their own affairs led by cadres recruited locally mostly from the poor peasants.

Furthermore, collectivization provided a foundation for China's industrialization by assuring high rates of accumulation (averaging early 30% for the years 1957–1980) and by enabling the state to transfer much of this rural surplus to urban industry and urban consumption as well as to foster rural industrialization. The combination of assured subsistence diets and the provision of basic health care enabled China to raise life expectancy to nearly 70 years by the end of the collective era (Kerkvliet and Selden, 1998, p. 45).

Collectivization has also raised peasant welfare to a new level. Different from pre-socialist villages, villages under socialist China arranged material assistance for needy members and families (the physically handicapped, the elderly, the children, etc.) as entitlements or rights, rather than as charities. Thus, the famous *wubao* (five guarantees) system was introduced in most of the collectivized farming communities. Financed from a collective welfare fund, this system provided some basic needs for a small number of needy persons and families in each collective. The contents of *wubao* varied over time and across regions. Food, clothing, and burial expenses were mostly included; fuel, school fees, medical care and housing were variably included. In the 1960s, the *wubao* system was expanded from seven guarantees (including food, clothing, housing, health care and sick leave, maternity benefits, education, and funeral and wedding ceremonies), to 10 guarantees (adding haircuts, entertainment, and heating), and even to 16 guarantees (adding lighting, tailoring, upbringing of children, transportation, a small marriage grant, and old-age care). Under the so-called three-tier system, the production team not only became the agricultural production unit, but also the basic unit of welfare administration (Chang, 2003, p. 153).

Finally, the collectivization legacy provided the much-needed rural infrastructure and local institution to carry out the post-1978 economic reforms. It was during the Maoist era that reservoirs were constructed, the irrigation system strengthened, and the drainage network improved. During the Great Leap Forward, the state mobilized millions of peasants to construct dams, reservoirs, and large-scale irrigation systems for the communes. It was also during the collectivization era that rural industries and enterprises were set up in the communes, local cadres accumulated managerial experiences through running commune and brigade enterprises, and local governments were asked to promote economic and social development in the rural communities. The collectivized policy provided the medium to tap local resources, mobilize underutilized rural labor, train local leaders, and arouse local initiative. Without all these infrastructure and institutional foundations built in the socialist era, it is doubtful whether agricultural productivity could have increased so rapidly in the early 1980s, and whether local village and township enterprises could have played the leading role in China's industrialization in the 1980s.

However, despite the above-mentioned remarkable achievement during the Maoist era, critics are quick to point out that China's collectivization experiment is not without problems. China's collectivization experiment was built upon the foundation of the Soviet developmental model which was biased towards rapid industrialization in the cities. Like its Soviet Union counterpart, China's urban-biased model relied upon siphoning the rural surplus to urban industry, primarily via compulsory grain sales at state-imposed low prices and secondarily through taxation (Cheng and Selden, 1994). But unlike the Soviet Union model, China set up a new *hukou* system to control the vast migration from the countryside to the towns and cities that rapid industrialization might generate. Especially, since the 1960s after the failure of the Great Leap Forward, China's party-state has erected a great wall between city and countryside, locking rural people into their villages and cutting off most of the remaining intra-rural and rural–urban exchange.

Therefore, despite the fact that class inequality was sharply reduced in the countryside and there was the homogenization of rural social class at the village level, there were still massive social inequalities between the countryside and the city. To a certain extent, class inequality and class conflict was transfigured spatially into a sharpened rural–urban divide, with surplus extracted from the countryside to promote rapid industrialization in the cities. As Lee and Selden (2007) point out, in socialist China under Maoism, the party-state "policed social divisions, manifested as differential entitlements, rights and income, particularly between collectivized villagers consigned to agriculture on the one hand, and urban workers and employees in state and collective enterprises on the other".

Benedict Kerkvliet and Mark Selden argue that the party-state's program of high extraction of agricultural surpluses had resulted in stagnation in rural income throughout the two decades of the collective era. Similarly, He Qinglian (2009) argues that low consumption and stagnant rural incomes in Mao's people's communes caused peasants to lose enthusiasm for collectivized production and the rural economy became impoverished. Two decades of rural poverty and widening of rural–urban gap may have laid the foundation for post-1978 capitalist reforms.

THE REMAKING OF THE MAOIST PEASANTRY SINCE 1978

In China's countryside, pressure against collectivization, which existed throughout the collective era, came to a head following the death of Mao in 1976. China's collective system guaranteed peasants' employment and subsistence, yet it also sustained vast rural under-employment and left many peasants in poverty and yielded few income gains.

Without fanfare, peasants in the late 1970s, sometimes supported by local and regional officials, pressed to expand the scope of household and market. Although Kate Zhou (1996) insists that decollectivization was a totally bottom-up process — what she calls a "spontaneous, unorganized, leaderless, non-ideological, apolitical movement", David Zweig (1997) points out that researchers need to strike a balance among peasant spontaneity, cadre interests and resistance, market reformers' views, as well as central policy disputes, all of which are necessary components of a full explanation for decollectivization.

Under the **"household responsibility system** (*baogan daohu*)**"**, all land was divided equitably among the peasant households in reminiscent of the land reform of the 1950s. Peasant households paid the state agricultural tax and took responsibility for the compulsory grain sales to the state. After that, the remainder of the produce was for the peasants to sell or consume. The only socialist aspect of this system was that land ownership remained as collective property vested in villages whose officials assigned user rights to peasants for extended periods like 30 years. In other words, peasants do own the land collectively, even though they cannot sell it in the land market.

The party-state was fully in charge of the decollectivization process. The redistribution of collective land in the form of household contracts coincided with a period of dynamic gains in the rural economy that peaked during 1978–1984 because the party-state encouraged agricultural diversification (ending "grain first" practices) and provided an immense boost to peasants in the form of increased agricultural purchasing prices. These measures stimulated agricultural production and increased rural incomes during 1978–1984, when agriculture achieved very impressive gains.

In addition, local authorities in China also sold, gave away or contracted to peasant households the farm machinery, draft animals, sideline enterprises and other means of production that the collectives had previously owned. Consequently, peasant households emerged as the primary locus of agricultural production and many other economic activities. Later, many peasant households, individually or at times jointly, started their own industrial, service, and commercial establishments and turned into rural capitalists. These kinds of capitalist activities are far more numerous, prosperous, and export-oriented in coastal China than in the country's inland areas.

In the 1980s, China's rural township and village enterprises (TVEs) were the most dynamic sector of the economy, a magnet for overseas Chinese investment, the largest source of new employment and income generation, and the cutting edge of China's rapidly growing exports and trade surpluses. TVE ownership is multilayered, involving not only township and village but at times also the county and higher levels of the state, sometimes entwined with private and even overseas Chinese capital.

However, despite decollectivization and the introduction of market incentives that succeeded in producing a sharp increase in agricultural production in the short term, they failed to provide a long-term solution to the problem of backwardness in the Chinese countryside. Indeed, in many aspects it was a step backwards and made the matter worse.

First of all, the breakup of the communes and the introduction of household responsibility meant that most peasant households ended up with plots of land that were far too small to allow for the efficient use of mechanization or the application of modern farming techniques. It also meant that basic infrastructure such as roads and irrigation system, whose upkeep had been the responsibility of the commune, fell into disrepair. Thus, although market incentives proved more effective than the old methods of socialist ideology and coercion in making peasants work harder, they failed to bring the modernization of the Chinese countryside.

By the mid-1980s, the spurt in agricultural output brought about by economic reforms had begun to peter out, leading to serious food shortages. These food shortages contributed to the economic and political crises of the late 1980s that led to the protests in Tiananmen Square in 1989. The problem of food shortage persisted well in the 1990s, and was resolved only when the rising export of manufactured products were able to provide the foreign exchange necessary to buy food from abroad.

It may be true that many peasants, who had the advantages of both being in close proximity to booming urban markets and having favorable connections with local party-state officials, had been able to transform themselves into capitalist farmers or rural capitalists in post-socialist China. However, this has not been the case for the vast majority of peasants who live in inland provinces or in areas far away from the urban cities. Indeed, the majority of peasants were to become worse following the introduction of market reforms. In the late 1980s, Wen Tiejun (2001) began to theorize and popularize the phrase *sannong wenti* (three rural problems), i.e., *nongmin* (peasants), *nongcun* (village), and *nongye* (agriculture). In the post-socialist era, peasants are now at the mercy of market forces and an economic policy which favors exports and cities over the countryside, leading to the bankruptcy of the peasants (poverty and widening of rural–urban gap), the bankruptcy of the villages (after the dismantling of the rural welfare system, the village governments are no longer able to provide basic services like health care, education, and welfare), and the bankruptcy of the agriculture (Chinese agricultural products cannot compete with foreign agricultural products after the entry to WTO).

The above bankruptcies forced the peasants to migrate to the cities to seek a living, leaving only the elderly and the children in the villages. Chan (2013) estimates that about 230 million migrants now work in the city; this migrant-worker labor force has supplied the global economy with the largest ever army of super-exploitable labor. This "unlimited" supply of cheap peasant migrant workers at the late 20th century laid the foundation for China's economic boom over the past 30 years.

THE FIRST WAVE OF PEASANT PROTESTS AGAINST TAXES AND FEES IN THE LATE 1980s

In response to the above peasant problems, we observed the emergence of the first wave of peasant protests in the 1980s. Thornton (2004, p. 87) cites a Chinese government report confirming that in 1993 over 1.5 million cases of protests occurred in that year alone, over 6,000 of which were officially classified as "disturbances" (*naoshi*) by the authorities. Of these cases, 830 involved more than one township and in excess of 500 participants; 78 involved more than one county and over 1,000 participants; and 21 were considered to be "extremely large-scale" events, involving more than 5,000 participants. A surprising number of these confrontations turned violent: these incidents of protests resulted in 8,200 casualties among township and county officials; 560 county-level offices were ransacked; and some 385 public security personnel were fatally injured. A different source reported that the number of public protests and demonstrations in China reached 110,000 in 1999 and 87,000 "mass incidents" in 2005 (*The Economist*, 2007). Although the reliability of these figures and the definition of what constitutes a "mass incident", a "protest", or a "disturbance" remains in doubt, it is certain that peasant protest is now quite a common phenomenon in the Chinese countryside since the 1980s.

There are several distinctive characteristics of peasant protests in post-socialist China. First of all, most of the protests took place in a township and were aimed at the abusive tax collection policy of the township government. Although the incidents might ostensibly appear to be anti-state, it must be stressed that the target was not the central government. In fact, peasants identified themselves with the center, and called upon it for help. In the 1990s, the peasants usually began their protests with the slogan "Resolutely unite around the Center of the Communist Party headed by President Jiang Zemin and Premier Zhu Rongji".

Moreover, village officials — part of local government — were often found within the leadership ranks of the protests, and they provided the peasant protesters with support (information, networks, and other resources). And despite the fact that violence and clashes had occurred during the protests, these were for the most part a result of provocation by the township government. Generally speaking, rural inhabitants wish nothing more than to undertake a protest that is peaceful, and to this end they start their action with a non-violent demonstration.

Examining all these reports of peasant protests in the Chinese countryside cannot but raise a number of questions. Why have so many rural "disturbances" arisen in post-socialist China? Why do peasants target the local township government but not the central state? Why do village officials themselves often join the ranks of those protesting against township government? What is the impact of such agrarian conflict on the Chinese state and the wider society? And how to interpret peasant protests in the framework of class and class conflict?

THE RISE OF LOCAL PREDATORY STATE

In post-socialist China, there has been a dramatic transformation in the structure of Chinese government, so as to facilitate the implementation of market-oriented reforms by local agencies. From that conjuncture, the central state apparatus has loosened its control over local affairs, and a wide range of decision-making powers devolved from the central government to the lower levels so as to promote local incentives. As a result, the local state apparatus acquired greater managerial power over public enterprises, more flexibility in local budgetary processes, increased freedom to approve foreign investment and engage in international trade, and expanded jurisdiction over resource distribution and taxation. With central authority gradually retreating from local administrative and economic affairs, local government has now taken over to become the engine powering capital accumulation.

In addition to administrative decentralization, the party-state also experienced fiscal decentralization. In the mid-1980s, provincial, municipal, county and township governments were subject to a bottom-up revenue-sharing system that required localities to submit only a portion of the revenues to the upper level. Lower-level tiers of government were permitted to retain all — or almost all — of what remained after this upwards payment had been made. This fiscal decentralization policy converted local states into financially independent entities that had the unprecedented right to dispose of the revenue they retained. Fiscal decentralization has had the following important effects on the Chinese state and society. First, it has led to a rapid increase in the size of and expenditure by local government, not least because it now has more economic resources under its control. As such, grassroots authorities at these lower tiers of government now pursued new economic ventures in the form of village and township enterprises. Second, fiscal decentralization has led to a significant decline in the financial oversight exercised by the central state and correspondingly weakened its extractive capacity.

By the 1990s, bureaucratic expansion of the local governments coupled with fiscal decentralization had created a budgetary crisis in nearly all the poorer counties, which experienced difficulties even in paying basic salaries. In these economically less favored regions, high non-discretionary outlays for personnel on the government payroll, including local officials, teachers, health workers, and other social service providers generally accounted for over half of local budgetary revenues (Lin *et al.*, 2006, pp. 314–315).

How were local cadres to fulfill their performance contracts and obtain the necessary resources to run the local state bureaucracy?

Apart from employing a range of creative mechanisms (such as deferring wages and cutting expenditure on social development) to cope with persistent fiscal deficits, local cadres might also resort to a number of predatory activities to generate additional income.

One way of generating additional sums was the widespread practice of what Gong (2006, p. 93) has termed "little money lockers" (*xiaojinku*), in which extra- and off-budgetary funds were hidden. With constraints on budget revenues as a result of the central state claw-back, the only way for local officials to obtain more financial resources was to generate irregular and sometimes illegal extra- and off-budgetary resources. In addition, local government imposes capricious surtaxes, fees, and fines on individuals, state and private enterprises. This has been categorized as the imposition of what might be termed the "three arbitraries" (Lin, 2002): (1) *arbitrary payments*, which refers to *ad hoc* fees collected on public goods and services: "public security fee", "garbage disposal fee", "road maintenance fee", "sanitation fee", "supervision fee", and "environmental fee"; (2) *arbitrary fines*, which include penalties on businesses or individuals for violating national or local laws and/or regulations, such as road occupation charges and penalties for defying family planning policy; and (3) *arbitrary exactions*, which entail compulsory contributions to various local government funds for public security, environmental protection, and retirement pensions.

What is startling is not just the irregular and capricious nature of these *ad hoc* appropriations, but also their extent, their unaccountable nature, and the ways that the resulting funds are spent. Wedman (2000) estimates that the total sum of irregular taxes, fees and other income collected by various governments exceeds Y100 billion (around US$12 billion) each year. Gong (2006) reports that enterprises in Hunan province were subject to more than 140 types of taxes and fees, while there were nearly 400 kinds of *ad hoc* fees in Wuxi city of Zhejiang province. Furthermore, the unaccountable nature of these off-budgetary funds enables local officials who levy them hugely to enhance their own living standards, adopting in some cases lavish patterns of consumption. Often these funds are used to finance tours abroad or to purchase luxury items (foreign cars), as well as provide expensive office furniture and housing as perks for individual officials.

These kind of activities underline the "predatory" nature of the local state, a behavior that Evans (1995, p. 44) has described as being able to "extract a large amount of otherwise investable surplus while providing so little in the way of 'collective goods' in return that they do indeed impede economic transformation". In a fundamental sense, the local predatory state mimics historical patterns, both the kind of appropriation effected and the methods used in furtherance of this. The difference is that in the past it was the landlord class that carried this out, whereas now it is the personnel of the local state. Insofar as the landlord class prior to 1949 was the local state, there is a fundamental continuity in this kind of practice.

This extraction of arbitrary fees and taxes on the peasantry has led to growing conflicts between local party-state officials and the peasants. This was to become worse with the economic retrenchment at the end of 1980s. By the 1990s, in some of the more remote districts, peasant insurrections began to break out in which the party-state officials were driven out of the autonomous areas established. In 1997, these insurrections began to reach a large-scale with armed uprisings breaking out in less remote areas in the central provinces of Anhui, Henan, Hubei and Jiangxi, each involving tens and thousands of peasant protesters.

By the end of 1990s, these peasant protests had reached a scale that, if left unchecked, could have seriously challenged the authority of the Chinese communist party. As a result, the Chinese party-state was obliged to take action. In addition to strengthening the repressive apparatus, the party-state announced a series of measures (like anti-corruption campaigns and local democratic elections) to defuse the situation. Finally, in 2004, the party-state announced that agricultural taxes were to be phased out over two years and extra state investment was made in furthering economic development in the remote regions. In 2005, proposals were put forward to provide a basic social security system for China's rural population. "Five Guarantees" were to be granted to the elderly, the unemployed, the disabled, and the children, ensuring that they would have regular supply of food and clothing together with a minimal standard of housing, medical care, and a decent burial.

As a result, the wave of peasant insurrections in the remote regions subsided in the late 2000s. The party-state has, therefore, been able to defuse peasant insurrections by spreading out some of the benefits of rapid accumulation of industrial and urban capital to the entire rural population. However, for many peasants in the more populated eastern and southern regions of China, rapid industrialization and urbanization over the past two decades have been more of a curse than a blessing. Since the late 1990s, there has been a new wave of peasant protests over the illegal land seizure, the expropriation of land and the conversion of agricultural land from cultivation to industrial and residential uses, and the degradation of the rural environment.

THE SECOND WAVE OF PEASANT PROTESTS AGAINST ILLEGAL LAND SEIZURE SINCE THE 1990s

Gilboy and Heginbotham (2004, p. 258) point out 168,000 cases of illegal land seizures were reported by the Ministry of Land Resources in November 2003, twice as many as in the entire previous year. The trend continued to accelerate, with some 2.54 million hectares, or 2% of total farmland, lost in 2003 alone. Some 34 million peasants have lost their land entirely since 1987, and the new surge in land transfers certainly indicates acceleration of that process. China's best-known business and economics magazine, *Caijing*, has called the recent wave of rural land seizure by local officials and real estate developers a new "enclosure" (*quandi*) movement. What then explains this new wave of illegal land transfers in the 2000s?

To start with, the new policies of the central state have not been able to solve the structural problem caused by fiscal recentralization: Local government bureaucracy remained overstaffed and in debt, and could not get enough resources to provide basic services to the peasant families. Local cadres are still expected to fulfill their performance pledges, meeting a set target of enterprise taxes, industrial output, and local development so as to bring in as much resources into the local area as possible.

In addition, economic boom in the past two decades has resulted in very rapid urbanization. Towns and cities have sprung up like mushrooms, their interactions have multiplied and their boundaries expanded. Subsequently, the countryside has transformed itself into urban landscape with booming rural and township enterprises. These parallel processes of *ruralization of the city* and *urbanization of the countryside* have blurred the boundary between town and countryside (Tang and Chung, 2002).

The problem of illegal land seizure is compounded by the "institutional ambiguity" regarding land ownership in the Chinese countryside (Ho, 2001, p. 400). The question "who is the legal holder of ownership" has never been clearly spelled out in the Chinese legal system. By law, the village collective has the right to use (*jingying*) and supervise (*guanli*) the use of land, but has no right to buy and sell this resource. The state, on the other hand, "may, in accordance with the law, expropriate land which is under collective ownership, if it is in the public interest" (Guo, 2001, p. 424). Thus, the power to carry out planning, supervision, expropriation and, most importantly, the transfer of land in the countryside is vested in township government. Lin *et al.* (2006) explain that how this institutional ambiguity and fiscal pressure has combined to generate a new wave of illegal land seizure in the Chinese countryside:

"In more developed regions where urbanization and industrialization contributed to raising land values, grabbing land from peasants became pervasive. Revenue-hungry city governments have every incentive to expropriate more agricultural land for urban expansion and commercial leases and make a profit since land revenues fall into the locally controlled extra budget. With faster urbanization and stronger regional competition for outside investments in this period, local governments initiated a wave of land requisition and established industrial parks and urban new-development zones." (Lin *et al.*, 2006, p. 320)

There is accordingly a strong financial incentive for township and village governments to engage in this kind of predatory behavior. The study by Guo (2001, p. 428) confirms that the bulk of income generated by land sales went to township government (60–70%) and to village government (25–30%), while peasant smallholders received very little compensation from such property transfers (only 5–10%). Moreover, income from the sale of land constitutes around 80% of extra-budgetary funds that accrue to a township-level government.

Again, the central state responded to this wave of local predatory behavior by formulating yet more policies, regulations, and institutions. In 2006, therefore, the central government created a new land Superintendence, dramatically increased oversight of land markets, and imposed new rules on those markets. These policies should in theory deprive local officials of crucial discretionary revenues and patronage resources obtained through selling farmland to urban developers (Naughton, 2007).

In addition to the expropriation of land, the peasants also suffered from the degradation of environment. With an overriding drive to accumulate capital, China's nascent capitalists have given scant regard to the environment. Local party-state officials regularly turn a blind eye to the breach of even the minimal environmental regulations set by the central government. As a result, many of China's industries pump out vast amounts of highly toxic pollutants with little restrain. Pollution has reached such a scale that it is causing serious health concerns on the part of the Ministry of Health. According to joint research by the World Bank and the Chinese government, there are an estimated 750,000 premature deaths due to respiratory diseases caused by air pollution. However, what is far worse is water contamination. With many of China's rivers turned into open sewers and conduits for industrial effluence, an estimated 700 million people drink contaminated water, with 190 million people suffering illness as a result (Economy, 2007). It is said that all along China's major rivers, villages report skyrocketing rates of diarrheal diseases, cancer, tumors, leukemia, and stunted growth.

As a result, pollution is fast becoming a major issue in China and there were more than 50,000 recorded pollution-related protests in 2005. Perhaps, one of the well-reported protests took place in the city of Xiamen in 2007. After months of mounting protests over the proposed construction of a petro-chemical plant, students and faculty members of Xiamen were reported to have sent out a million text messages calling on their fellow residents to protest (Economy, 2007). The bulk of protests against pollution have been conducted by peasants because it is the peasants who have borne the brunt of the environmental impact of pollution and environmental degradation. For example, industrial pollution contaminates land and spoils crops. It is estimated that as much as 10% of China's agricultural land is polluted. In addition, China's peasants have to compete with growing industrial demands for water. Even when the peasants obtain water to irrigate their crops, it is often contaminated (Economy, 2007).

THE FORMATION OF A BIFURCATED STATE

From a peasant's perspective, central government is "benign" because it cuts taxes to relieve the peasant's burden and increases financial transfers to expand social services to local areas. Moreover, this positive view of the central state apparatus is reinforced by the repeated attempts of the Beijing government to strengthen regulations protecting the peasantry from "exploitation" by corrupt local officials and greedy urban developers. On the other hand, township government is perceived by those at the rural grassroots as "malign: not only does the local state impose excessive taxes and fees on the peasantry, it also takes the side of urban developers so as to enrich itself by dispossessing peasants of their land".

Compared with other authoritarian regimes in the third world, the top leaders in the communist party-state are generally perceived by the Chinese peasantry as having people's interests in mind, while the local authorities are blamed for what goes wrong in peasants' daily lives (Huang, 2013).

Guo (2001, p. 435) reports that when peasants complained about land expropriation, escalating tuition fees, rising education surcharges, and the deterioration of irrigation and the environment, they always consciously differentiated the local government from the central government:

> The central policies are good and in favor of us peasants. But when they reach the provincial level, the policies have gone out of shape. The further down, the more distorted the policies become. By the time they reach the village, the policies have completely changed from what they were in the first place.

Guo (2001, p. 436) further explains the formation of a bifurcation state as follows: The state with which the peasants normally interact is local: the township government. In this structural setting, the relationship of the peasants with the central state is mostly political and symbolic, whereas the relationship with the local state is social and economic. The relationship between the central state and the peasants is maintained at a moral level, whereas that between the local state and the peasants is more tangible and tied to interests in concrete terms. For this reason, the competition for control over economic resources (like land) between the peasants and the local state under the influence of neoliberal capitalism has become a major source of conflict in the Chinese countryside.

Obviously, this split between *a 'benign' central* and *a 'malign' local state* has profound implications for the pattern of agrarian conflict, including the target, the discourse, the strategy, the leadership, and the outcome of peasant protests. Unless the split nature of the state is inserted into the analysis, it is impossible to clearly understand why peasant unrest is directed only at the township but not at the central government, why village cadres often join such protests, and why this kind of rural agency is unlikely to result in political upheavals and regime transition.

THE PATTERN OF PEASANT PROTESTS AT THE END OF THE 20TH CENTURY

Drawing upon their findings on the first wave of peasant protests against taxes and fees, Bernstein (2004), Thornton (2004), Perry

(2007), O'Brien and Li (2006) have pointed to the following characteristics of the peasant protests at the turn of the 20th century.

The Target of Peasant Protests

Among the different levels of government, it is the township government that bears the brunt of peasant anger. As the study by Guo (2001, p. 437) indicates, township government was the main target of village protests, not least because it was the authority that issued notifications of land expropriation, and the ones who deprived villagers of their land by force were township government officials. In short, both the local state and its staff are the most visible evidence for — and thus the clearest manifestation of — oppression and dispossession experienced by the Chinese peasantry.

Why township officials were invariably singled out in peasant protests is attributed by Bernstein (2004, p. 11) to the fact that the former were under intense pressure to extract funds, both for career reasons and because townships generally were greatly dependent on such economic resources. Given their role in enforcing land expropriations, the physical presence of township officials at the point of conflict also intensified and reproduced the antagonism which subsequently fueled villagers' resistance (Guo, 2001).

On the other hand, the central government never appears on the peasants' complaint list and is never directly attacked in peasant protests. Quite the opposite, the central government is often seen as the "ultimate savior" of the Chinese peasant; seeking allies at higher levels of the state is clearly the main strategy of peasant protests. As such, it seems our Chinese case fits nicely with Eric Hobsbawm's (1997, p. 202) observation that "people at the grassroots level confined their struggles to fighting those oppressors with whom they had immediate contact".

The Discourse of Peasant Protests

In keeping with the pattern of this appeal starting from lower levels to authorities at the upper levels, O'Brien and Lianjiang (2006) have coined the term "rightful resistance" to describe peasant conflict in the Chinese countryside. Rightful resistance is to defend the rights already granted by the central government, yet often denied by local officials, or rights that peasants believed could be derived from the regime's policies, principles, and legitimating ideology. In the course of undertaking such protests, Chinese peasants endeavor to persuade local officialdom that they — the peasants — are engaged in an entirely legitimate behavior.

According to Shue (2004), however, Chinese peasant discourse in protests represents an artful means using the "grammar" embedded in a system of domination to utter statements that raise doubts about the system. For example, peasants use out-dated norms, such as the 1960s Cultural Revolution-era "four freedoms", to justify putting up big-character posters to expose cadre corruption. Thornton (2004, p. 98) also notes that Maoist revolutionary language — like the slogans "return land and property to the peasants!" and "Long live the peasant communist party!" — is frequently brought back to justify peasant protests. However, while they are shouting the Maoist revolutionary slogans, peasants also make it clear that they are loyal to the present "capitalist" communist party too and put up a poster like "Resolutely unite around the Center of the Communist Party headed by President Jiang Zemin and Premier Zhu Rongji" during their protests.

The Strategy of Peasant Protests

The term "boundary-spanning contention" is used by O'Brien (2004) to support the contention that Chinese peasants desire to exploit the gap between rights promised by the central state and rights delivered at the local level. In order to protect themselves, and simultaneously to improve the chances of success, peasant protesters tender impeccably reasonable demands and profess little more than a wish to make the system live up to its promises (what it is supposed to be). This caution, O'Brien points out, is bolstered by the fact that claims made by those protesting are limited in scope. That is, they are doubly circumscribed: parochial and local (i.e., defending the interests of a particular community) protests at the rural grassroots never seek to be national and operate outside what exists politically.

Peasant protests, then, involve "boundary-spanning claims" that sit near the fuzzy boundary between official, prescribed policies and forbidden ones, in a middle ground that is neither clearly transgressive nor clearly contained. Peasants who engage in this type of contention characteristically combine lawful tactics (e.g., collective petitions, seeking audiences with power-holders) with disruptive but not quite unlawful action, e.g., silently parading with lit candles in broad daylight to symbolize the "dark rule" of local leaders. Chinese peasants always behave in accord with prevailing statutes (or at least not clearly in violation of them), and they use the regimes' own policies and legitimating myths to justify their action.

As a rule, the center is more tolerant and better intentioned than local power officials, which makes it convenient for rightful resisters to invoke commitments from above ignored by local officials.

Furthermore, peasant protesters can find allies, even patrons at higher levels of the state, as the latter are usually eager to uncover and stop misconduct of their local agents. O'Brien and Li (2006, p. 65) say "divisions in a multilayered state with formidable principal-agent problems thus made rightful resistance possible". The Chinese peasant protesters are especially skillful in exploiting such an opportunity after growing up in such a political structure.

The Leaders of Peasant Protests

Village officials often show up as leaders of peasant protests against the township government. They contribute personal and family networks, organizational expertise, as well as financial resources to peasant protests. Having local government officials is crucial in explaining the emergence and the persistence of peasant protests in the Chinese countryside over the past three decades. As such, why lower-level government officials are willing to participate in public protests against a higher-level government in this manner?

To a certain extent, this action can be interpreted as a product of "rightful resistance". Village government officials legitimated their roles in peasant protests by claiming that they were acting in the name of the Center; they were only opposing those township officials who had grossly violated central policies. They saw themselves as upholding the interests of the Communist party-state, which were not separable from the peasants' legitimate rights and interests (Bernstein, 2003, p. 8).

Thornton and Li, however, offer an economic explanation. Highlighting the market dimension, Thornton (2004, p. 90) argues that "market reform policies have tied the interests of local cadres, managers, and administrators more firmly to the financial soundness of the collective work unit or local community, and have made them less dependent upon the central state".

Focusing on the village elections, Li Lianjiang offers a third democratic explanation. Li (2002, p. 104) argues that "free and fair elections seem to have made villagers more willing to urge cadres to resist township's decisions that contravene central policies and harm village interests…. Free and fair elections may give them [villagers] an organizational resource to deploy in their struggle with predatory local governments".

The Impact of Peasant Protests

In light of the fact that Chinese peasants have a dual concept of the state and that peasant struggles are consequently mainly of the type classified as "rightful resistance" which seldom goes beyond what is permitted opposition, it is highly unlikely that agrarian conflict will lead to political upheavals and regime changes in China.

However, it is also misleading to assert that peasant conflict would not result in any significant impact on macro structural changes in the Chinese society, politics, and economy. For example, two decades of rightful resistance against local taxes and fees, as O'Brien and Li (2006, p. 124) observe, have "gradually, directly, but surely … spurred a policy change, namely, a reduction of the fiscal burden". Indeed, it could be argued that the transition from neoliberal capitalism to state neoliberalism is itself the outcome of widespread peasant protests. However, since there is also no political upheaval and the present communist party-state is not under imminent danger of an agrarian revolution, the source of macro structural changes has to come from the top through the state elites rather than from the bottom through the peasants.

In addition, peasant conflict is significant because it helps to generate a new generation of Chinese peasants who possess right consciousness (O'Brien and Li, 2006; Thornton, 2004), who are willing to participate in political action to defend their rights, and who are experienced in exploiting political openings in the state to protect and expand their interests. At present, the rights' consciousness of Chinese peasants is still highly rudimentary and is mostly state-orchestrated (Perry, 2007). However, if peasants continue to take part in political resistance, their right consciousness could be raised to such a level that could lead to the development of class consciousness.

THE CHANGING PATTERN OF PEASANT PROTESTS IN THE SECOND DECADE OF THE 21ST CENTURY

In the early 21st century, Jianrong Yu (2010) began to talk about a new pattern of peasant protests in the Chinese countryside. First of all, after land conflicts became the focal problem, the intensity of resistance has been steadily increasing, with the number of "mass incidents" sharply increasing from 8,700 in 1993 to over 180,000 in 2010.

Second, there is the emergence of skillful protest organizers, leading to a more organized resistance. O'Brien (2009, p. 26) explains that chronic resistance is a produce of "skilled protest organizers who know how to shape claims, mobilize followers, orchestrate act of defiance, and (occasionally) mount actions that transcend the borders of a single community. … In the face of long odds, these activists have regularly tested the truth of the saying, "A big disturbance produces a big result, a small disturbance produces a small result, and no disturbance produces no result".

Yu (2010) reports that peasant protesters in Hunan have formed a peasant association to organize their protests in 2002. Spontaneous village organizations like "Burden Reduction Group", "Committee of Peasant Autonomy", "Committee for Reducing Burdens" or "Burden Reduction Monitoring Group" have been formed during peasant protests (Yu, 2010; Walker, 2008). However, Yu (2004) points out that due to the ban of the communist party-state, these spontaneous peasant organizations rarely keep any written record or documentation. Most of the protests are carried out by word of mouth instead of by written records. Nor do they assign any specific posts to members and are especially careful in appointing formal leaders.

Third, the peasant activists tend to adopt more spirited defiance in their protests. Learning from their past experience, they concluded that comparatively tame forms of contention (lodging complaints to higher level of government) are ineffective, and that forceful, attention-grabbling tactics (such as blocking a road or organizing a sit-in) and confrontation tactics (such as surrounding fee collectors or a prelude to driving them off) are needed.

Fourthly, violence is also on the rise. O'Brien (2009, p. 26) reported a number of clashes between the peasant and local authorities have taken place in early 21st century over issues such as locating a power plant on village land, or refusing to allow the recall of corrupt officials. More than a few of these incidents have led to significant casualties after armed police or local toughs arrived to repress the protesters.

In addition, Jianrong Yu (2008) has documented the spread of unplanned, "accidental" protests that rapidly take on a life of their own. These so-called *anger-venting* flare-ups are often sparked off by essentially random incidents (e.g., the rumor that a street vendor has been seriously beaten by a rich person or a policeman or a minor street scuffle between a porter and an individual claiming to be a government official). An example of an "anger-venting" incident is the "Weng'an riot" in June 2008 which involved tens of thousands of residents in Weng'an County in Guizhou province of Southwest China. Rioters smashed government buildings and torched several police cars to protest against an alleged police cover-up of a girl's death. Participants joined in on the spot, even if their interests were not directly implicated. Such flare-ups may reflect the underlying class contradictions in both rural and urban China and an aggrieved class of dispossessed peasant migrants and laid-off workers. The protesters and rioters are merely venting their frustrations, feelings of resentment, and anger because they are upset at the local authorities and at the rich people.

Fifthly, three new groups — lawyers, environmentalists, and mafia — were found to be heavily involved in the peasant protests in the 21st century. Yu (2010) explains the entry of these three actors in agrarian conflict as follows: many lawyers now become involved in land conflicts because they could reap huge economic benefits from the lengthy legal cases against the wealthy developers. Environmentalists are involved because recent land conflicts often implicate the theft of subterranean resources (such as forests and mines) and rural environmental problems (such as the pollution of agricultural land and nearby rivers). Mafia is involved because the corrupted local authorities need them to snatch the peasant's land. Kathy Walker (2006) used the term "gangster capitalism to describe the plundering of public wealth by power-holders and their angers-on and He Qinglian (2006, p. 93) reported that "local governments throughout China have used criminal organizations as goon squads to force urban residents from their homes and seize farmers' land".

Despite the above new characteristics, the second wave of peasant protests against land grab still shares the following traits with that of the first wave of peasant protests against taxes and fees. First of all, the protesters' concerns are still about economic issues, not political issues. In the early 21st century, the peasants wanted more monetary compensation about their loss of land; they were not interested in political issues, like transforming the local power structure or building a new local government.

Second, their protests continue to be within the confines of "rights resistance" and they seldom go beyond the limit allowed by the communist party-state. As O'Brien (2009, p. 27) points out, "rural protest plays a role in fending off extraction, deflecting predatory behavior and sending unpopular cadres packing, but there is little evidence that it poses an imminent threat to the communist regime".

Third, the peasant protests continue to focus more on reactions to inappropriate policy or action of the developers or local officials, and less about moving a cause forward. Currently, even though the peasant protesters are more skillful in organization and mobilization, they seldom possess an alternative vision on how to empower themselves to protect their interests and lifestyle.

Finally, even though there are more lawyers and public intellectuals involved in peasant protests, as O'Brien (2009, p. 27) points out, "most contention remains weakly organized, and cooperation across class lines is still rare". As a result, claims tend to be circumscribed and popular action is usually small-scale and localized. There are few signs of solidarity, score, and coordination that a sustained peasant movement would require.

CONCLUSION

In coming to power, the communist party-state had brought important changes to class relations in the countryside. In the early 1950s, the land reform policy equalized land ownership within villages, eliminated tenancy and hired laborer, broke the power off the dominant landlord class, and improved the livelihood of small owner-cultivators. The post-1956 collectivization drive transferred authority over labor, land, and production process from peasant household to cadres and local party-state. Thus, class inequality was sharply reduced in the Chinese countryside and there was the homogenization of rural social class at the village level during the socialist era in the 1950s–1960s. However, there were still massive social inequalities between the countryside and the city. To a certain extent, class inequality and class conflict were transfigured spatially into a sharpened rural–urban divide, with surplus extracted from the countryside to promote rapid industrialization in the cities.

The post-socialist era since 1978 started with the "Household Responsibility System" through which all the land in the village was sub-divided among the peasant households in reminiscent of the land reform of the early 1950s. Since then, peasant households emerged as the primary focus on agricultural production. The breakup of the communes and the emergence of the household responsibility system meant that most peasant households ended up with plots of land that were far too small for mechanization. It also meant that basic infrastructure such as roads and rural irrigation systems, whose upkeep had been the responsibility of the commune, remained in disrepair. Indeed, the majority of the peasants, especially those who are living in inland provinces or in areas far away from the urban cities, were to become worse after the introduction of market reforms. In post-socialist China, peasants are now at the mercy of market forces which favors exports and cities over the countryside, leading to the bankruptcy of the peasants (rural poverty and the widening of the rural–urban gap), the bankruptcy of the villages (the local governments are no longer able to provide basic services like health care, education, and welfare), and the bankruptcy of the agriculture (Chinese agricultural products cannot compete with foreign agricultural products).

Such bankruptcies have forced the peasants to migrate to the cities to seek a living, thus leading to increasing unrest in the Chinese countryside. The first wave of peasant protests was against the extraction of arbitrary fees and taxes by local government officials, while the second wave of peasant protests was directed against the rural land seizure by local officials and real estate developers. From a peasant perspective, there is a split between the central government and the local government. The central government is "benign" because it cuts taxes to relieve the peasant burden and increases financial transfers to expand social services to local areas. On the other hand, the local (township) government is perceived by those at the rural grassroots as "malign: not only does it impose excessive taxes and fees on the peasantry, it also takes the side of urban developers so as to enrich itself by dispossessing peasants of their land".

The formation of a bifurcated state has led the peasants to adopt a "rightful resistance" discourse in their protests. Rightful resistance is defending of rights already granted by the central government, yet often denied by local officials, or rights peasants believed could be derived from the regime's policies, principles, and legitimating ideology. Peasants also adopt a "boundary-spanning" strategy to exploit the gap between the rights promised by the central state and the rights delivered at the local level. Chinese peasants always behave in accord with prevailing statutes (or at least not clearly in violation of them), and they use the regimes' own policies and legitimating myths to justify their action. The Chinese peasant protests seldom go beyond the official boundary tolerated by the central government.

Despite land grabbing producing a second wave of peasant protests in the early 21st century, and despite peasant protests now becoming more widespread, better organized, more confrontational, more violent, and involving more actors (like lawyers, environmentalists, and mafia) than before, the communist party-state and its bifurcated state structure still exert a strong influence on the pattern of peasant protests. Peasant protests continue to be narrowly economically driven; they seldom go beyond the limit tolerated by the central government; they tend to be reactive rather than proactive; the peasants still do not have a strong link to the urban working class or to the new middle-class public intellectuals.

As such, it seems that the Chinese peasant has not yet formed a class to protect its class interests. Although the Chinese peasants started to protest against the arbitrary exactions of fees and taxes and the illegal land seizure by the local state officials, they couched their resistance in the language of "rights resistance" while professing little more than a desire to make the system live up to what it is supposed to be as promised by the central state. Their rights' discourse and right consciousness can hardly be transcended to a higher level of class discourse and class consciousness because they complained only about the individual *agents* (corruption of individual local officials and individual greedy developer) instead of the *structure* (the collusion between the local state and the capitalist class).

Moreover, they tend to take the existing post-socialist structure for granted. They are not challenging the authority of the communist party-state or the logic of capitalist accumulation; they just want the local state officials to extract less arbitrary taxes and fees or the real estate company pays a high amount of compensation to their collective land.

Furthermore, the Chinese peasants have yet to develop their own class organization and their own leadership. Their village organization is controlled by the communist party-state and peasant protest leaders are often drawn from village officials. These peasant leaders justified their protests in the name of the central government while upholding the interest of the party-state; they were only opposing those local township officials who had grossly violated central policies.

Although the Chinese peasant has not yet developed class consciousness and formed a class organization, the prospect for an independent peasant class cannot be ruled out in the future. If post-socialist development in China would trigger more acute class contradiction in the countryside (like the recent push to large-scale farming and agribusiness (Zhang and Donaldson, 2008) and the speeding up of the urbanization of the countryside, and the land seizures had destroyed peasants' livelihoods and basis for survival), if there will be more opportunity of forming a class alliance between the new middle class public intellectuals and the peasantry like in the recent "New Rural Reconstruction Movement" (Wen *et al.*, 2012), it is possible that the Chinese peasantry could be more assertive in promoting its class interests in the 21st century.

Chapter 8

THE MAKING OF A NEW MIDDLE CLASS

"It is a well-known fact", as Hagen Koo (1999, p. 86) points out, "that class boundaries of the middle class are inherently fuzzy and theoretically controversial. Numerous attempts at conceptual precision and unending debates among class theorists have not brought us closer to a consensus in defining middle class and drawing its boundaries in a clear fashion". In the literature, S.M. Lipset (1963) and Samuel Huntington (1991) have added more confusion by including both the *capitalists* (who own property, exercise authority, and extract economic surplus in production relations) and the *educated professionals* (like lawyers, technicians, and mid-level managers who hold a higher education degree, do not own any productive assets, and are dependent on a monthly salary for their livelihood) into the middle class.

To avoid confusion, this chapter focuses upon the *new middle class* who are educated salaried professionals whose superior market situation (income, job security, occupational prestige, etc.) is mostly derived from their higher education credentials, professional expertise, and authoritative position rather than from their ownership of private property. Thus, members of the new middle class include such urban professionals as physicians, engineers, university professors, and mid-level managers and administrators in the party-state.

This chapter will start with a review of the literature on the democratic potential of the Chinese new middle class. Then, it will discuss the nature of the new middle class in socialist China (1949–1978). After that, it will study the emergence of new middle class politics in the post-socialist period (1978–the present). Finally, this chapter will discuss whether the new middle class can promote democratization in China.

THE LITERATURE ON THE CHINESE NEW MIDDLE CLASS'S DEMOCRATIC POTENTIAL

The China field has presented a contradictory view on the democratic potential of the new middle class. On the one hand, the Chinese middle class is said to be "conservative" and "moderate". Jonathan Unger (2006, p. 31) argues that "the Chinese educated middle class has become a bulwark of the current regime". Unger warns: "do not expect regime change or democratization any time soon. The rise of China's middle class blocks the way". He Li (2003, p. 88) similarly concludes that "the new middle class as a whole does not pose any significant threat to the current regime. It quietly endorses the leadership in Beijing". Examining the case of home-owner's resistance in the cities, Yongshun Cai (2005, p. 777) also reports that "the Chinese middle class is largely moderate because of its intention to maintain the political order and limited ability to stage disruptive action".

On the other hand, a democratic orientation is usually found from the surveys on the attitudes of the Chinese middle class. For example, Tang *et al.* (2009, p. 91) find that "Chinese middle class has a greater degree of democratic orientation on all aspects". When people say that they belong to the middle class, they choose to identify with such "pro-democratic values like individualism, pluralism, and liberalism, and recognize their responsibilities to facilitate progressive social political changes". In another survey conducted in Beijing, Jie Chen and Chunlong Lu (2006, p. 2) also find that "Chinese middle-class individuals, especially in an urban setting, do think and act in accordance with democratic principles".

What explains the above contradictory views of the Chinese middle class? One possible explanation is the literature has used a different level of analysis. The survey findings are based on an individual-level analysis, while other studies conduct their investigations at a higher structural level. It is possible that members of the middle class exhibit attitudes of democracy and talk democratically, but they have a different behavior when they act collectively as a class. As such, this chapter aims to go beyond an individual-level analysis by focusing on how the middle class acts collectively as a class to protect its interests and lifestyle.

A DEPENDENT, RESTRICTED NEW MIDDLE CLASS IN SOCIALIST CHINA

In pre-revolutionary China, the state sector was small and most of the new middle class professionals were employed in the private sector. After the 1956 nationalization drive in socialist China, however, employment opportunities outside the state/collective sector had virtually disappeared and state employment became the norm. Nevertheless, the new middle class experienced an expansion, rather than a contraction, because the nascent socialist party-state urgently needed the highly educated to fill the many new technical, professional, and managerial positions created in the state sector.

Despite its increase in size and playing a more important role in economic development, China's urban new middle class had suffered much in Maoist's revolutionary China (Davis, 2000). Not only had the new middle class lost private resources and physical mobility, but they also had lost the ability to accumulate the social and symbolic capitals that define and defend distinctive class boundary. As a result, the new middle class was totally dependent on the communist party-state in every sphere of life and experienced humiliation and violent attacks during the Cultural Revolution.

Three aspects are critical for the formation of the new middle class: First, *Class Organization*: The new middle class must be able to secure resources independent of the state and engage in associational activity to protect its class interests. Second, *Class Identity*: The new middle class must be able to develop a peculiar pattern of taste, consumption, or style of life in order to consolidate support and commitment from its members, and distinguish itself from other classes. Third, *Class Reproduction*: Since the new middle class is characterized by its possession of high educational credentials and professional expertise, the new middle class must be able to transfer these traits to its second generation in order to attain class reproduction. However, during the period of revolutionary socialism, China's new middle class had failed to make any advances on the above three critical aspects.

First of all, after the elimination of the private sector in 1956, the urban new middle class professionals almost immediately became a stratum of salaried civil servants in the party-state. After they graduated from college, they were assigned professional jobs by the party-state under a unified rational state plan. They could not refuse their job assignments because there were simply no jobs available in the private job market. Rather, they needed to be obedient to their CCP superiors because the party-state defined the rules for occupational advancement and monopolized the venues for professional activities. Furthermore, they were not encouraged to develop horizontal ties to their non-party professional peers. Unable to establish professional organization of their own or even to establish recreational clubs outside the party-state, new middle class professionals and managers found it difficult to build linkages across the boundaries of their work units and develop social network among its members (Davis, 2000).

Second, due to their low standards of living in socialist China where they lived in the public housing in the work units, members of the new middle class's consumption pattern and lifestyle were quite indistinguishable from that of the working class. Especially during the Cultural Revolution, any member of the new middle class who put on make-up, wore a Western style of dress, or decorated his/her home well were seen as committing "bourgeois crimes" and they became targets of attack by the Maoist revolutionaries. During the Cultural Revolution, new middle class members were criticized as "intellectual aristocrats who rode on the working people. They thought they were knowledgeable; actually they were the most stupid because their knowledge had no use to the working class whatsoever. They should be reborn through continuous criticism and self-criticism. They should tuck their tails, be obedient pupils to the masses" (Deng and Treiman, 1997, pp. 399–400). Therefore, the new middle class was deprived of the opportunity to cultivate its own lifestyle, to develop its own symbolic capital, and to draw its own class boundary separated from the working class.

Finally, on the critical issue of class reproduction, the Chinese party-state tried a variety of ways to promote educational opportunities for the children of peasants and working class backgrounds at the expense of those from the new middle class, e.g., the party-state not only abolished tuition fees, provided students with subsidies, and guaranteed jobs following graduation, but also set up preferences for students from desirable working class and peasant class backgrounds (Deng and Treiman, 1997). During the Cultural Revolution, recruitment examinations were abolished. The major criteria for college admission became class background and party loyalty rather than academic achievement (Shirk, 1982). The only eligible applicants were "workers, peasants, and soldiers with two or more years of working experience". Thus, it is very difficult for China's new middle class to have class reproduction during the Cultural Revolution.

In sum, the new middle class was severely curtailed, both politically and economically, after the Communist revolution. It became a *dependent, deformed* class in socialist China during the 1950s and 1960s. This class had been totally incorporated into the party-state's civil service and completely controlled by the party-state in every sphere of its activities. However, the new middle class has experienced a dramatic come back in post-socialist China.

THE FORMATION OF THE NEW MIDDLE CLASS IN POST-SOCIALIST CHINA

Over the past few decades, China's remarkable economic development, together with the drastic expansion of its higher education system, has led to a profound transformation of its economic and social structure. In post-socialist China, a higher education degree has become the key credential for people to gain entrance to the new middle class's professional, managerial, and technician jobs.

Whereas in the 1980s, only 2–4% of the age cohort could attend university; in the 2010s more than 23% were able to attend. In 2013, it is expected that three in five young Chinese graduates from high school would attend college, matching the United States of the mid-1950s. In the first decade of the 21st century, China doubled the number of colleges and universities to 2,409 and quadrupling its output of college graduates (Bradsher, 2013). This rapid expansion in higher education, coupled with urbanization and the growing number of new middle class jobs, has led to the very rapid growth of the new middle class in the 21st century (Lin and Sun, 2010, p. 238).

Since the Chinese new middle class has emerged during the post-socialist era a couple of decades ago, it belongs to the first generation and still has not yet attained a clear-cut identity and pattern of behavior to distinguish itself from other classes.

Nevertheless, by the turn of the 21st century, the Chinese mass media and the foreign press began to talk about a new collective identity called "the middle class" (*Zhongchan Jieji*), "middle stratum" (*Zhongjianceng*), or "middle-income stratum" (*Zhongjian shouru jieceng*) (*CHINADaily*, 2004; *Phoenix TV*, 2006; *The Economist*, 2002; Li, 2010). Focusing on the income level and the consumer power, the mass media reported that a middle class member was earning a monthly salary of 5,000 Yuan in 2004 and by this benchmark more than 80 million Chinese people could be categorized as the middle class. The mass media also optimistically projected that within 10 years, some 400–500 million Chinese would enjoy a "middle income", making China's consumer market much bigger than that of the United States.

From the mass media's perspective, the Chinese new middle class began to form at the *cultural* level, as distinguished by its unique pattern of consumption and life style. Thus, members of the new middle class are reported to live at high-priced residential neighborhood, own the property they live, drive their own automobiles to work, use credit cards to shop at branded departmental stores, join overseas tours, send their children overseas for education, hire a helper at home to take care of the mundane household chores, take elaborate efforts to decorate their homes in the gated community, and safeguard their privatized, individualized lifestyles (Liu, 2009; Li, 2010; Zhang, 2010).

Apart from the above cultural formation, the new middle class also began to participate at the political front and they are getting more active in the following three political activities.

First of all, the middle class is getting more active in their *professional association* activities through voicing their professional interests and raising other political issues. In post-socialist China, professionals were allowed to form their own association after they received blessings from the party-state. When the All China Lawyers Association (ACLA) was first set up in 1986, it was aimed to be a legal organization to enforce rules of conduct, professional ethics, and professional competence on its lawyer members. However, over the past few years, ACLA began to venture beyond its professional boundary and raise all sorts of issues that have far-ranging implications.

In 2005, 100 lawyers put forward a petition at the Sixth Annual Meeting of the ACLA to demand the Public Security Office to remove the barriers (like bars and wires) that separated the lawyers from their clients in the Public Security meeting rooms. The lawyers framed their petition not only as a means to defend "lawyers' rights", but also as a means to defend their "clients' rights". The lawyers said their clients should be considered as innocent until they were proven guilty by the court. They said that the Security Office was wrong in treating the arrested persons as criminals, denying them the rights of communication with their lawyers. By framing their petition as a right-defending issue, the lawyers not only challenged the authority of the Public Security officials, but they also helped to expand the legal rights of the Chinese citizens.

Apart from this petition to remove barriers from the Public Security Office, the ACLA proposed other laws to expand the legal rights of Chinese citizens. For example, the ACLA proposed a new slavery law to protect coal miners and other people who are put into a slave-like condition. They also proposed a new competitive law to protect the rights of consumers from a powerful phone company that had monopolized the communication market.

Second, members of the new middle class joined *social movements* to articulate their concerns and protect the lifestyle and interests of their members. Homeowner's resistance movement, for instance, is a means to defend the consumer rights of the new middle class, to safeguard the new middle class's privatized lifestyle, and to protect the autonomy of the new middle class community (Liu, 2009). Homeowner's resistance movement frequently draws upon the essential resources of the new middle class, like lawyers' familiarity with private property laws, architects' design knowledge about building construction, managers' sophisticated negotiation skills, former state officials' extensive interpersonal networks and contacts with the news media. With these new middle class resources behind the movements, homeowners in a middle class neighborhood could win battles against powerful developers and corrupt local officials. These battle victories, in turn, have greatly empowered the new middle class.

Similarly, when intellectuals (including writers, scholars, scientists, other professionals, and college students) become more vocal in their demands for a cleaner environment, these new middle class demands are very hard to suppress with the result that the Chinese environmental movement has been gaining strength over the past two decades. As environmental activists often expose the institutionalized corruption and the lack of accountability of the entire system of governance, many new middle class environmental activists have expanded their demands and become closely linked with democracy activists who agitated for broader political reforms (Economy, 2005; Lee *et al.*, 1999).

Third, there is a *pre-existing democratic party* route in new middle class politics. Several small democratic parties were formed before 1949, and they are tolerated because the Chinese communist party (CCP) put forward a united front policy of multi-party cooperation and political consultation under the leadership of the communist party. For example, the China Democratic National Construction Association (CDNCA) is one of the small democratic parties that has been in existence before the reform era. By 2008, CDNCA had 114,347 members in 361 local branches. The members include a large number of intellectuals and professionals working in the private and the public sectors. In 2008, CDNCA had a total of 17,363 members represented in various levels of the National People's Congress (NPC) and Political Consultative Conference (PCC). With such a large representation in NPC and PCC, CDNCA is also getting more active, providing a variety of opinions and voicing many new ideas at the NPC and PCC meetings. Some of these opinions and ideas of CDNCA include: to reduce poverty, to develop the non-public sector, to strengthen the links with the Hong Kong and Macao professionals, etc.

Through the above three routes (the professional associations' route like the ACLA, the new social movements' route like the home owners' resistance movement, and the pre-existing political parties route like the CDNCA), the new middle class is beginning to emerge as a political actor, voicing its concerns and participating in Chinese politics in order to protect its interests and lifestyle.

THE NEW MIDDLE CLASS'S MODE OF POLITICAL PARTICIPATION

Although the Chinese new middle class has just emerged and its political formation is highly rudimentary, it has presented a unique mode of political participation that is different from the other classes. In general, the new middle class's political participation has the following characteristics: moderate, high-tech mobilization, and stay within the existing state limit.

First, the new middle class's political participation tends to be *rational and moderate.* It is willing to engage in negotiation and compromise, and it tries to avoid violent confrontation with other classes or the state. Because the new middle class is resource-rich (they have professional expertise, extensive social network, and negotiation skills), they need not resort to such radical actions as blocking the highway and engaging in violent demonstrations in order to attain their goals.

Second, members of the new middle class tend to use *new communication technologies* (internet bulletin board, web blogs, SMS wireless service, etc.) to mobilize their members for collective action. They need not resort to face-to-face mobilization at the community level because they are at the cutting edge of high-tech development, and they highly value privacy and respect individual autonomy (Liu, 2009).

Third, the middle class often *acts within the state limits*, because they are better educated and always rational to use the existing legal channels. As Cai (2005, p. 779) points out, the middle class is "fully aware of the boundaries of state tolerances; fear of punishment compels them to take action acceptable to the state". In homeowner's resistance movement, for example, lawyers are usually involved in waging collective lawsuits against the developer or the management company because the home owners want to ensure that their protests are within limits set by the party-state. The new middle class can afford to go through lengthy legal processes because their economic resources and their professional expertise enable them to do so.

Fourth, the new middle class's politics tend to take the form of *voice* as in speaking out of their own interests, giving advice and opinions on policies, appealing for the demands on behalf of other classes or groups through legal channels (litigation), the mass media (newspapers and TVs), and the internet.

In passing, I want to point out that 300 middle class members signed a document entitled Charter 08 in December 2008. The document calls for an entirely new constitution, an independent judiciary, direct elections, freedom of religion, speech and assembly, and the right to form independent political parties in China (Ramzy, 2008). Although a small radical segment of the new middle class could be quite critical to the party-state and call such structural transformation as democratization, the new middle class as a whole is quite moderate, avoids taking a confrontation position, tends to use the existing institutional channel to articulate its concerns and works inside the party-state, and feels contented merely to have a voice.

As such, why the Chinese new middle class is so contented with the existing institutional structure and seldom challenges the communist party-state?

THE NEW MIDDLE CLASS AND THE PARTY-STATE

During the socialist era between the 1950s and the 1970s, the new middle class had an uneasy relationship with the party-state in China. The Communist Revolution was founded on the support of workers and peasants, and the communist party-state did not trust the middle class. In the Hundred Flowers Campaign and the Cultural Revolution, many new middle class members were humiliated, downgraded, and sent to the labor campus in the countryside for re-education.

However, the communist party-state has drastically changed its relationship with the new middle class during the post-1978 reform era. In 2002, the Chinese party-state called for "enlarging the size of the middle-income group" (Li, 2010, p. 11). Instead of taking a hostile stand, the communist party-state is now friendly with the new middle class, as shown by the following processes.

To start with, the party-state's post-socialist reform policies during the past three decades are in harmony with the interests of the new middle class. Policies such as the expansion of higher education institutions, the setting up of high-tech developmental zones, attracting foreign investment, and adopting an export-led industrialization strategy naturally would enhance the interest of the new middle class because China will need more professors to teach in the universities, more engineers to work on the machines and construction industry, more scientists to work in high-tech industries, more lawyers to handle the legal complications in forming business partnership with foreign corporations, more social workers to handle the social problems created by the sudden shift from a state-socialist economy to neoliberal capitalism, etc.

In addition, the party-state has adopted policies that are particularly aimed to boost the well-being of the new middle class. For example, during the past two decades, the state has raised the salary of the university professors several times so the Chinese professors' income now is much higher than that of the average urban workers. University professors are also given very generous housing benefits, such as they could buy an apartment from their work unit (*danwei*) at a discount price or they are given generous housing allowances so they could buy or rent accommodation at a very nice middle-class neighborhood (Liu, 2009).

Luigi Tomba (2010) has pointed out that housing subsidization of the party-state has played a very important role in the upward mobility of the new middle class. The housing careers of new home-owners had often been kick-started by the subsidized acquisition of a *danwei dwelling*, by the access to subsidies to buy a second apartment, by the access to credit through the "housing provident fund", or through the use of the *danwei* apartment as collateral in a mortgage agreement. Beijing is probably among the clearest cases in which the local party-state has used housing policies to boost consumption and build a broad-based, high-consuming, professional new middle class.

Moreover, unlike the situation in Maoist China where the new middle class had to keep their mouth shut or risk political prosecution, the new middle class now feels that they have a voice which is respected by the state officials and the party leaders. Members of the new middle class are often recruited into the think tank or invited to join the consultation committees to advice or voice opinions. Irrespective of whether their opinions are accepted by the party-state or not, members of the middle class feel they are highly respected by the party-state because they have a chance to participate in the decision-making process and believe they could influence policy-making through the existing political channels (Dong Fang Zao Bao, 2005).

Finally, there is a "fusion" between the new middle class and the communist party-state. On the one hand, there is a *professionalization of the party leaders* and *state cadres*. For example, in 2006, it was reported that out of the 35,637 communist party members in Beijing Xuanwu District, 12,989 (or 36.5%) had the educational qualification of post-secondary or university education (Beijing Xuanwu District, 2006).

In order to encourage the professionalization of state officials and party leaders, the party-state implemented a policy of bureaucratic promotion and recruitment: An applicant who has a BA degree will be appointed as a member; an applicant with a master degree will be appointed as Vice Head; while an applicant with a PhD degree will be appointed as Head of the department (Beijing Xuanwu District, 2006).

Besides, the party-state also invests a lot of money in sending the cadres to advanced nations (like the U.S.) to undergo training. Guangdong Province, for instance, is reported to have spent 100 million yuan in five years to send 300 higher-level cadres overseas for training. The Guangdong government requires that the overseas trainer must be less than 47 years old if he/she is a city-level cadre, must have a university BA degree, and must have a foreign language proficiency equaled to a four-year university level. The media reported that upon return from their overseas training, the cadres feel more professionalized and more confident in managing their departments (Nan Fang Du Shi Bao, 2003).

On the other hand, members of the new middle class are being recruited into the communist party-state. As the communist party has maintained a high degree of support in the Chinese society, university students are not deterred to be a member of the communist party as it could provide an advantage in the job market in both the private and public sectors. Similarly, university graduates and professionals are attracted to enter the state bureaucracy because it has instituted a policy which favors the hiring of the applicants with a BA, a Master, and a PhD degree (Nanping Shi, 2004).

TOWARD A QUIET DEMOCRATIZATION?

This chapter traces the transformation of the new middle class politics in China. In the socialist era during the 1950s and 1960s, the new middle class was a dependent and deformed class totally at the mercy of the communist party-state. However, in post-socialist China since 1978, the new middle class has experienced a dramatic expansion in size and in influence.

This chapter argues that rapid economic development in post-socialist China has led to the expansion of the new middle class in China. At the turn of the 21st century, a new middle class began to form not only at the cultural front (as shown by the gated community and by the affluent lifestyle and consumption) but also at the political front. The new middle class is becoming more active in politics through the following three routes: First, *the professional route,* as the middle class professional associations began to raise wide-ranging concerns that often go beyond their professional boundary. Second, *the social movement route,* as the bulk of leaders and members of the social movements come from the middle class. Third, *the existing political party route,* as the bulk of leaders and members of the existing small democratic parties come from the middle class and these small democratic parties are becoming more active in voicing their concerns over different issues.

Examining the above routes of political participation show that the Chinese new middle class tends to adopt a rational and moderate position and it tries to avoid confrontation with the state and other classes. It also tends to work within the limits set by the party-state and uses the existing institutional channels to voice its concerns and grievances.

The new middle class adopts the above modes of political participation because it has developed a good relationship with the party-state. Apart from the fact that the party-state's reform policies are in harmony with the interests of the new middle class, the party-state also sets up many specific policies that are aimed to enhance the interests of the middle class. Thus, the new middle class is the beneficiary of the reform era and has a stake in the preservation of the present social order, and that is why it is a supporter of the communist party-state.

Besides, there is a fusion between the party-state and the new middle class. On the one hand, there is *the professionalization of the party leaders* and *state officials.* On the other hand, the new middle class are recruited into the party-state. If this trend continues, the communist party-state will soon become a new middle class party-state in several decades; its members are mostly drawn from educated professionals who are proud of their educational credentials, technical expertise, and organizational authority.

What is the implication of the above analysis for the prospects of democratization in China? In developing countries, democratization emerged when the authoritarian state was overthrown by the noisy protests on the street, in which the new middle class acted as leaders and organizers of the "noisy" democratization revolution. The third wave of democratization that Huntington (1991) talks about is full of examples of this *noisy democratization.*

However, it is obvious the Chinese situation is different. Despite the Chinese new middle class getting more politically active, despite incidences of mass disturbances in the countryside and in the cities, and despite many pundits' predictions that communist party-state would fall after the 1989 Tiananmen Incident, there is little sign to show that the democracy movement is becoming alive again and the communist party-state is losing its mandate to rule.

It seems that China will not take the route of "noisy democratization", given the fact that the new middle class is moderate and rational and there is a fusion between the new middle class and the party-state. It seems unlikely that members of the new middle class would turn themselves into democratic martyrs, sacrificing their superior market condition, high status, and comfortable lifestyle to fight and die for the cause of democracy.

But does the new middle class need to adopt a confrontation stand to promote a democratic revolution in China? Does the "communist" party-state need to be overthrown in order to have a multiple-party free election in China? Does democratization in China need to go through a revolutionary phase with open, violent confrontation and abrupt, radical structural changes?

If the above analysis is correct, the Chinese new middle class is actually in a good position to push for another mode of democratization, what can be called a *quiet democratization,* in China. Over the past decade, the new middle class has been voicing political issues, raising concerns, and setting up new practices (like expanding the rights of citizenship, implementing the rule of law, enlarging the scope of civil society, pressing more accountability and transparency from the party-state) that are important in laying the groundwork for democratization.

The mode that the new middle class is following is also conducive to democratization. The new middle class's moderate, non-confrontation stand shows that it shares with the communist party-state's goal of political stability and avoiding class polarization, and therefore, it is not a threat to the party-state. Thus, the party-state would see the new middle class as its chief supporter and ally. Coupled with the fusion of membership between the party-state and the new middle class, the new middle class will gradually have a stronger voice on policies. As times go by, the party-state policies will gradually reflect the agenda of the new middle class.

In sum, instead of taking a confrontation position to impose democratization on the party-state from below, the new middle class has been quietly laying the groundwork for democratization by working from within the party-state. If the party-state feels empowered by the professionalization of the cadres of the party-state, if the party-state thinks that it has gained strong societal supports from the Chinese citizens, and if the party-state does not feel any threats of its survival from outside forces, then it is foreseeable in the near future that the party-state could initiate democratization from above so as to consolidate its basis of legitimacy. Should such an event take place, a quiet democratization will emerge in China without any open, noisy confrontation like the third wave democratic revolution that happened in the Philippines, Korea, and Eastern Europe.

It seems that Mary E. Gallagher (2002, p. 371) also shares the above argument, as she states, "There may be benefits to delay political change in China. Integration into the global economy, the increased use of legal institutions to mediate conflict, and the influence of a small but growing middle class may together slowly build up a more stable societal foundation for democratization".

Since the new middle class has only recently emerged, it may be too early to say anything definitive about its impact on Chinese politics. It is also hard to make any prediction in social science because the future is highly contingent of the choices that the actors are making at the present. However, irrespective of whether the above structural trend is promising, certain unforeseeable historical events like the global financial crisis and dramatic economic slowdown in the Chinese economy may derail the new middle class project of quiet democratization.

FUTURE PROSPECTS

The cordial relationship between the new middle class and the party-state is contingent on the latter's pro-new middle class policy, i.e., whether the party-state is able to deliver rapid economic development, promote the expansion of middle class occupations, and safeguard the affluent lifestyle of the new middle class. The new middle class, so far, has supported the post-socialist party-state because its members enjoy advances in their professional careers, upward mobility with respect to their family background, and freedom in pursuing their individualized, privatized lifestyle. However, all these class privileges may come to an end if China's remarkable economic development is not continued.

Since 2008, China has not been able to immune itself from the global economic crisis. In 2012, the official growth target for China was lowered to 7.5%, down from the 8% that had been set as a minimum target in recent years. China's export sector was hit hard by sagging demands from overseas, and its domestic performance was undermined by weaknesses in the important property sector (Wassener, 2012).

Li (2010, p. 11) reports that according to certain sociologists in China, the Chinese new middle class has actually been shrinking in recent years, partly due to the loss of jobs and financial assets as a result of the global financial crisis and partly due to the rapid rise in housing in urban China. With the tightening of the job market during the economic slowdown, the unemployment rate among college graduates (who are presumed to be member's of China's new middle class) is growing. College graduates are frustrated because not only they cannot get good jobs but they also face the challenges of rising housing prices and rising costs of services. There is great uncertainty, therefore, as to how many of them can actually make it into the ranks of the new middle class (Lin and Sun, 2010, p. 230).

The new college graduates have earned themselves a nickname, *fengqing* (literally, angry youth). These young Chinese "often use the internet to vent their frustrations, and that frustration often comes from either their patriotism or their desire to seek what is right, fair, true, and transparent. They care about social issues. And they feel they need to be outspoken, to have their voices heard. And they often use the internet to gain knowledge and have their voice heard" (Lin and Sun, 2010, p. 235).

Similarly, Zhang Li reports that in recent times, the new middle class in China tends to be more cynical about policy promises made by the authorities, more demanding about government policy implementation, and more sensitive as regards to corruption among officials. In addition, Zhang reports that if the voices of the new middle class are suppressed, if their access to information is blocked, or if their space for social action is confined, a political uprising is likely to take place (Li, 2010, p. 74).

Sociologist Sun Liping believes that the skyrocketing housing prices in large cities in both the coastal and inland regions have greatly enriched the real estate lobby but severely hurt the interests of newlywed, middle-class, who is increasingly unable to pay their mortgages. This explains why the television series "Dwelling Narrowness" (*woju*), which depicts the middle-class struggle in coastal metropolitan cities, became one of the country's most popular series in 2009 (Li, 2010).

The growing number of protests carried out primarily by members of the new middle class may reflect the increasing likelihood of the emergence of this *angry middle class*. Examples include the protest against a plan to build 11 billion yuan chemical factory in Xiamen in 2007, the urban resident movement that blocked the construction of new subway lines in Shanghai in 2008, and the middle-class neighborhood gathering (organized via the micro-blogging service Twitter) that prevented the building of a waste incineration power plant in Guangzhou in 2009. In all these cases, self-identified middle class protesters succeeded in pressing the party-state to alter course. These protests may reflect "a sign of the rising middle class" to redefine their social contract between the educated professionals and the party-state in the initial phase of post-socialist development.

Chapter 9

CONCLUSION

Using a historical approach, this book traces the social origin and the historical transformation of the class and class conflict in post-socialist China since 1978. It has found that the communist party-state has played a very decisive role in restructuring social classes and managing the emergent class conflict in Chinese society during the socialist and the post-socialist eras.

Chapter 2 examines how the Chinese socialist experiment has destroyed the old social classes and created the problem of new class in the Maoist era. Since the property-based definition was no longer useful to define social classes after the party-state had abolished private ownership, the Leftist Red Guards in the Cultural Revolution formulated a new **power-based definition** in order to attack the emergent new class in the party-state. The Leftist argue that the party-state has evolved into a new ruling class and has developed its own interests that are antagonistic to the interests of the peasants and workers. Thus, it is the control of the state apparatus, not the control of the means of production, which defines the new class in socialist China. According to the Maoist red guards, the power holder in the party-state is said to be the new ruling class or the "capitalist". The new class is characterized by its extraction of surplus from the state machinery (either legally or illegally through corruption), enabling the new class to get access to special resources and life chances, to live an extravagant life style that is distinguished from the masses, and to pass its class privileges to its offsprings. Thus, bureaucrats themselves form a class, with interests sharply antagonistic to those of the workers and peasants. Chapter 2 argues that the new class analysis in post-1956 China, especially during the 1966–1975 Cultural Revolution, has made the concept of class more individualized, politicized, and behaviorized; thus, class concept becomes an overloaded tool which can explain any social conflict, it exists everywhere and continues forever. It is this elusive new class definition that has deeply divided the Chinese society, resulting in numerous factional struggles and random violence.

Chapter 3 examines the impact of the reintegration in the capitalist world economy and the subsequent neoliberal turn on China's social classes and class conflict. The critical transition began in 1978 when Deng Xiaoping, the leader of the Chinese Communist Party took the first momentous step towards the liberalization of a communist-ruled economy. The path that Deng defined was to transform China in two decades from a closed socialist planned economy to an open center of neoliberal capitalism in the global economy. The first decade of neoliberal reforms, however, had led to serious economic and social problems in the Chinese society, triggered off robust democracy protests at the Tiananmen Square in 1989 to challenge the rule of the Chinese Communist Party. Chapter 3 argues that China has pursued a different mode of neoliberalism — a different form of configuration of class–state relationship what can be called ***state neoliberalism*** — from the mainstream neoliberalism that is promoted in the Washington Consensus model. The deepening of neoliberal reforms in the 1990s led to many different kinds of class conflict in society, as shown by the growing numbers of labor protests, peasant demonstrations, social movements, other large-scale social disturbances and by the increasing call to regulate the market. In light of the above class contradictions and discontents, the Chinese communist party-state began, in the late 1990s, to reverse its neoliberal policies and started to build up a developmental state. After the party-state strengthened its fiscal capacity through "Tax Sharing Scheme", it engaged in debt-financing investments in huge mega-projects to transform infrastructures and declared a new policy of "building a new socialist countryside" to address the issues of poverty and class inequality in the rural areas.

After reviewing the developmental policies which have significant impact on class and class conflict in both the socialist and the post-socialist era in the first two chapters, the rest of the book will examine the making of the Chinese capitalist class, the working class, the peasantry class, and the new middle class.

Chapter 4 discusses the formation of a hybrid **cadre–capitalist class** in post-socialist China. It has shown that the legacies of the Cultural Revolution and a strong Leninist party-state have played a decisive role in the making of the capitalist class. Since the economic foundations and political capacity of the capitalist class were completely eroded during the Maoist period, the old capitalist class was not able to seize the opportunity of the post-1978 economic reforms to revitalize itself. As a result, an *embourgeoisement* of cadres has taken place through the processes of local state corporatism, corporatization of state enterprises, and cadre engagement in private businesses. At the same time, nascent capitalists outside the bureaucracy needed cadre patrons, not only to help them to get access to market and bank loans but also to fend off the predatory activities of corrupt cadres. Through the processes of embourgeoisement of cadres and the *patronization of capitalists*, a fusion of political capital, economic capital, and social/network capital in local society has taken place, leading to a formation of a powerful cadre–capitalist class. By the late 1990s, the cadre–capitalist class had begun to take visible form, exhibiting a lifestyle of conspicuous consumption, establishing class organizations at the national, provincial, and local class levels, and starting to call for constitutional revision and more political representation in order to expand their class interests. Nevertheless, the formation of the cadre–capitalist class has occurred side by side with growing class differentiation, class polarization, and class conflict. Consequently, class conflict has emerged, with cadre–capitalists being challenged by almost all other classes. Cadre–capitalists have been attacked as corrupt, rent seeking, selfish, abusive of their political power, and wasteful of the country's economic resources for private conspicuous consumption. In the battle for legitimation, cadre–capitalists have tried to reinvent themselves as hard-working, nationalistic entrepreneurs and have developed a close working relationship with the party-state through political incorporation.

Chapter 5 argues that post-socialist economic reforms have done great harm to the Chinese **urban working class** in terms of job security, wages, and entitlements (such as housing, health care, and education). Subsequently, the urban working class responded by engaging in protests, and the number of labor protests have significantly increased over the past two decades. However, all these massive labor protests have failed to produce a nationwide labor movement because the party-state has played a decisive role in shaping the contour of labor insurgency in China. For example, the party-state has created deep social divisions in the working class, has prevented the working class from forming its own organization, has set up labor legislations to pre-empt labor protests, has pushed the protest towards the direction of "subsistence struggles", has punished middle-level officials in order to maintain a moral ground. In addition, a booming economy has greatly facilitated the state to impose an ideological hegemony over the workers, making the workers to blame themselves rather than making claims on systemic change.

Chapter 6 examines the making of the **migrant working class** in South China, the locale where China has become the world factory at the turn of 21st century. The literature has presented a very depressing picture of the migrant working class, pointing out that the migrant workers are powerless to defend their own interests. The migrant working class is absorbed in taking *individual* action about personal gains and losses, but has seldom taken any *collective* action; that is, it has not taken any action to improve the working conditions of the entire working class in South China. In addition, it is mostly focused on narrow *economic* issues (such as wage nonpayment) and it generally fails to raise any *political* issues (such as challenging arbitrary factory discipline) in the factories. Although it occasionally rises up in protest, it takes the existing institutions for granted rather than challenging their legitimacy. Although the migrant working class experiences brutal exploitation at work, it has a *muted class consciousness* and it identifies itself as a peasant rather than as worker. In summary, the migrant working class has not yet formed a "class" in a Marxist sense, and it is merely a class in itself, but not a class for itself.

However, Chapter 6 argues that migrant workers in South China have been drastically transformed in the first decade of the 21st century by the formation of a new generation of Chinese migrant working class and by the global capitalist crisis in 2008. Not only do they identify themselves as workers, but they also use the perspective of class to explain their experiences and sufferings. Their struggles have also moved beyond bread-and-butter economic issues; their mobilizations are no longer trapped by "cellular activism", producing several strike waves in different locations, and they increasingly see the need to go beyond the legal channel to pursue strikes and work stoppages in order to protect their class interests.

Chapter 7 examines the transformation of **the peasantry**. The breakup of the communes and the household responsibility system in China's post-socialist transition meant that most peasant households ended up with plots of land that were far too small for mechanization. It also meant that basic infrastructure such as roads and rural irrigation systems, whose upkeep had been the responsibility of the commune, fell into disrepair. Indeed, the majority of the peasants, especially those who are living in inland provinces or in areas far away from the urban cities, were to become worse after the introduction of market reforms. In post-socialist China, peasants are now at the mercy of market forces which favored exports and cities over the countryside, leading to the bankruptcy of the peasants (rural poverty and the widening of the rural–urban gap), the bankruptcy of the villages (the local governments are no longer able to provide basic services like health care, education, and welfare), and the bankruptcy of the agriculture (Chinese agricultural products cannot compete with foreign agricultural products). The first wave of peasant protests in the 1990s was against the extraction of arbitrary fees and taxes by local government officials, while the second wave of peasant protests since the 2000s was directed against the rural land seizure by local officials and real estate developers. From a peasant perspective, there is a split between the "benign" central government and the "malign" local government. This is because the central government cuts taxes to relieve the peasant burden and increases financial transfers to expand social services to local areas, while the local state not only imposes excessive taxes and fees on the peasantry but also takes the side of urban developers so as to enrich itself by dispossessing peasants of their land. This bifurcated state has led the peasants adopt a "rightful resistance" discourse and a "boundary-spanning" strategy in their protest, and their protests seldom go beyond the official boundary permitted by the central government.

Chapter 8 traces the transformation of **new middle class** in China. It argues that rapid economic development in post-socialist China has led to the expansion of the new middle class in China. At the turn of the 21st century, a new middle class began to form not only at the cultural front (as shown by the gated community and by the affluent lifestyle and consumption) but also at the political front. Examination of the mode of political participation shows that the Chinese new middle class tends to adopt a rational and moderate position and tries to avoid confrontation with the state and other classes. It also tends to work within the limit set by the party-state and uses the existing institutional channels to voice its concerns and grievances because it has developed a good relationship with the party-state. Apart from the fact that the party-state's reform policies are in harmony with the interests of the new middle class, the party-state also sets up many specific policies that are aimed to enhance the interests of the middle class. Thus, the new middle class is the beneficiary of the reform era and has a stake in the preservation of the present social order, and that is why it is a supporter of the communist party-state. In addition, there is a fusion between the party-state and the new middle class. On the one hand, there is *the professionalization of the party leaders and state officials*. On the other hand, the new middle class are recruited into the party-state. If this trend continues, the communist party-state will soon become a new middle class party-state in several decades; its members are mostly drawn from the educated professionals who are proud of their educational credentials, technical expertise, and organizational authority. Thus, Chapter 8 argues that the new middle class is actually in a good position to push for another mode of democratization, what can be called a *quiet democratization* in China.

The above-mentioned chapters have traced the historical emergence and transformation of class and class conflict in post-socialist China since 1978. They show that the many social classes — like the hybrid cadre–capitalist class, the migrant working class, and the new middle class — emerged during the post-socialist transformation over the past three decades. Due to their recent origins, these social classes are still undergoing a process of formation. They still have not formed their own class organization, developed a distinctive life style, and carved out a clear-cut class boundary from other social classes. As such, an interesting research question is whether they will become an agent to shape historical change and structural transformation.

For example, given the prevalence of labor insurgency and agrarian conflict in recent years, will the working class and the peasantry become agents for revolutionary transformation? Although the Chinese workers and peasants have begun to show their class antagonism toward post-socialist development, there is still a long way to go before they could be transformed into an historical agent of revolution. Over the past few decades, they still have not developed a strong independent class organization; their leaders still lack a vision and a coherent strategy to protect their class interests; and their protests are seldom sustainable to last a long period of time and extend to other locations. It seems highly unlikely that the insurgent class conflict from workers and peasants could propel China to a proletarian or a peasant revolution.

As such, will China move towards the path of a capitalist revolution? As China is experiencing rapid economic development and is fully integrated into capitalist world-economy, the influence of the market segment (which has little linkages to the party-state) in the capitalist class is bound to increase. At some point in the near future, the market segment in the capitalist class will want to complete the "unfinished business" of the neoliberal capitalism and have a clean break with the communist party-state in search of its own class agenda. For example, the market segment and "the liberals" within the communist party-state in early 2013 talked about rolling back the growing dominance of the state and state-owned companies over the Chinese economy, economic opening of more markets to competition, and ending the practices that allow state-owned (or state-blessed) companies to command cheap access to capital, resources, and land (Cohen, 2013). The market segment of the cadre–capitalist class would want to improve China's legal system and make it more transparent, more predictable, and more accountable. In sum, the market segment of the capitalists would want a "free-trading" market system and the setting up of capitalist infrastructure including the protection of property rights, clear boundaries between the state and the market, open and transparent information, etc. (Garnaut, 2013).

The new middle class, too, seems to be on the rise and has been more vocal than before in articulating political issues, raising concerns, and setting up new practices that are important in laying the groundwork for citizenship, human rights, and democracy. For example, in early 2013, the anti-censorship street protests against the crackdown of *Southern Weekend* by writers, lawyers, actors, and public intellectuals in the southern city of Guangzhou and in the online outrage that exploded over an extraordinary surge in air pollution in the north are demanding something that challenges the very nature of the communist party-state: transparency in the state bureaucracy, the public's right to know, investigative reporting and professional journalism, and the freedom of speech and the press (Shu, 2013, Wong, 2013). As one of the communist party-state's most ardent supporters, it seems the new middle class has the potential to influence the communist party-state towards its own class agenda.

As such, will China be moving toward the path of democratization? The prospect for the capitalists to become an ascending class and the rise of new middle class power in China is unlikely. Since the capitalists and the new middle class have only recently emerged, it may be too early to say anything definitive about their impact on Chinese politics. In addition, the emergence of the capitalist and the new middle class professionals took place under very unfavorable historical conditions.

First of all, as soon as the capitalists re-emerged in 1980s and 1990s, there were also the rise of intensive acute class conflict from the workers and the peasants in the Chinese society. The nascent cadre–capitalist class is seen as corrupt, rent-seeking, selfish, and abusive of their political influence, and wasteful of the country's economic resources. The cadre–capitalists are still struggling to re-invent themselves as nationalist entrepreneurs making significant contributions to the Chinese economy and society.

Moreover, the rise of the cadre–capitalists and the new middle class also took place in a period of uncertainty when the capitalist world-economy experienced wide fluctuations since the 2008 global financial crisis. If an economic boom helps the communist party-state to contain and defuse working class protests, an economic downturn of the Chinese economy could intensify labor insurgency leading to massive layoffs and drastic reduction in wages. If this happens, the new middle class could feel squeezed by the rising unemployment rate among college students. Young middle class professionals could feel frustrated if they not only cannot find good jobs, but also face the challenges of rising housing prices.

However, despite the insurgency from the workers, peasants, and the new middle class, the Chinese communist party-state is not under any serious threat. Instead of facing any danger of imminent regime collapse, the communist party-state is indeed highly stable. This book argues that the communist party-state is pretty successful in responding to the challenge of class conflict in the Chinese society. First of all, most of the class conflict is deflected towards the local party-state, with the protesters blaming the predatory local state officials of their social and economic problems while the central party-state is seen as benign and thus able to maintain a moral high ground. It also imposes political repression to disorganize the working class and the peasants. It bans any unofficial organization developed by the workers and peasants themselves, leading to a pattern of "leaderless" and spontaneous protest which tend to have short duration and not sustainable. It sets up many labor laws to individualize, to economize, and to pre-empt labor protests. Finally, it adopts the tactics of accommodation to diffuse working class protests if workers are willing to stay within a legal boundary that is tolerated by the communist party-state.

Moreover, there are also a fusion of their personnel between the communist party-state and the nascent capitalist class and the middle class professionals. Through the *embourgeoisement of cadre,* many state officials turned themselves into profit-seeking market actors running their own extensive business empires. On the other hand, through *the patronization of the capitalists,* the capitalists find a state official to provide them with vital business information, to get them to access to credit, raw materials, and markets, and shield them from arbitrary and irregular taxes. In return for the favors received, capitalists offer shares and partial ownership to their bureaucrat patrons. Since 2001, the recruitment of capitalists into the communist party has solidified or institutionalized the bonding between cadres and capitalists. The new middle class, too, has experienced a fusion with the communist party-state through the *professionalization of party leaders and state officials.* Higher educational credentials are built into the recruitment and promotion of officials in the state bureaucracy, and the communist party-state has invested a lot of resources in sending their cadres overseas to undergo professional training.

In sum, despite there widespread class conflict among the workers, the peasants, and the new middle class over the past three decades, the Chinese society is highly stable and the communist party-state has so far been able to contain, defuse, and institutionalize the class conflict.

Thus, it is unlikely that the working class and the peasantry will soon turn into the historical agent to promote a proletarian or a peasant revolution. Likewise, it also seems unlikely that the capitalists and the new middle class will turn into the historical agent to promote a bourgeois, democratic revolution. On the other hand, the communist party-state, due to its capacity to manage class conflict and its fusion of personnel with the capitalist class and the new middle class, is highly stable and it seems it is destined to stay in power at least for the time being. Thus, I agree with Friedman's

(2012) observation that at present a profound power asymmetry exists between the communist party-state and the insurgent social classes. Workers and peasants resist haphazardly and without any vision and strategy, while the communist party-state respond to the challenge of class struggles in a self-conscious and coordinated manner.

The above conclusion, nevertheless, should not be taken as presenting a favorable picture that the Chinese communist party-state is so powerful that it could suppress the revolutionary impulses and that China has become a harmonious society as portrayed in the official China media. Quite the contrary, the acute class contradictions which are released by the post-socialist neoliberal reforms are built into the socio-economic structure and thus are endemic. These structural contradictions will be forever present if China moves towards the path of neoliberal capitalism. There are bound to be numerous "mass movements" and class conflicts, some of which are growing in larger scale, moving towards greater intensity and getting more violent.

Moreover, the above optimistic conclusion about the stability of the present communist regime is based upon the assumption that China's remarkable economic development will continue. As a result, the party-state is highly resourceful and can buy off the protesters if necessary. Rapid economic development also provides numerous opportunities for social mobility, and the workers and peasants can solve their problems through individual means without challenging the existing power structure (Whyte, 2010). This explains why the class conflict in China tends to be highly economistic, with workers wanting more wages and peasants wanting a higher share of compensation over their land seizure. As long as the party-state is resourceful and is able to buy off protesters, it will be difficult to raise the economistic class conflict to a higher level which calls revolutionary transformation of the existing power structure.

However, since post-socialist neoliberal transformations have largely eroded the legitimacy of the communist party-state, now the communist party-state's legitimacy is mainly derived from its economic performance and its ability to raise the living standard to its citizens (so-called performance-based legitimacy by Breslin (2007, p. 44). If China ever runs into any unforeseeable economic breakdown or a prolonged economic slowdown, this will inevitably reconfigure the asymmetrical power relations between the communist party-state and the insurgent social classes. In this scenario, conflicts in Chinese society will be intensified and the social classes will become more vocal and militant than before, while the autonomy and the capacity of the communist party-state will be considerably weakened. As such, the prospect for revolutionary changes in the post-socialist China are contingent upon whether the communist party-state in China could continue its remarkable path of economic development and move away from neoliberal capitalism in such a way as to soften its structural contradiction of growing class inequality and class conflict.

REFERENCES

ACFTU (All China Federation of Trade Unions) (2010). Research report on problems of the new generation of Chinese migrant workers (in Chinese). *Xinhua Wang.* Available at http://news.xinhuanet.com/politics/2010-06/21/c_12240721.htm. Accessed on May 26, 2013.

Andreas, J (2012). Industrial restructuring and class transformation in China. In *China's Peasants and Workers: Changing Class Identity*, B Carrillo and DSG Goodman (eds.), pp. 102–123. Cheltenham, UK: Edward Elgar.

Aufheben (2008). Class conflicts in the transformation of China. Aufheben, 16. Available at http://libcom.org/library/class-conflicts-transformation-china [accessed on July 22, 2012].

Barboza, D (2009). Obama begins first visit to China. *The New York Times*, November 16.

Becker, J and M Elfstrom (2010). *The Impact of China's Labor Contract Law on Workers.* Washington, DC: International Labor Rights Forum (ILRF).

Beijing Xuanwu District (2006). *Year Book of Beijing Xuanwu District*, pp. 151–152. Available at http://xwnj2006.bjxw.gov.cn/06XWNJxxxsh.ycs?GUID=388080. Accessed on May 26, 2013.

Bernstein, T (2004). Unrest in rural China: A 2003 assessment report. *CSD working papers*, University of California. Available at http://repositories.cdlib.org/scd/04-13. Accessed on May 26, 2013.

Blecher, MJ (2002). Hegemony and worker's politics in China. *The China Quarterly*, 170, 283–303.

Boon, B (2006). Class struggle in China: A rise like a violent wind. Part I and Part II. *In Defense of Marxism*, April 10. Available at http://www.marxist.com/class-struggle-china-violent-wind100406.html [accessed on April 15, 2012].

Bradsher, K (2013). Next-made-in-China boom: College graduates. *The New York Times,* January 14.

Breslin, Shaun (2007). *China and the global political economy.* New York: Palgrave Macmillan.

Browne, A and N Shirouzu (2010). Beijing pressures Japanese on wages. *The Wall Street Journal,* August 29.

Cai, Y (2002). The resistance of Chinese laid-off workers in the reform period. *The China Quarterly,* 170, 327–344.

Cai, Y (2005). China's moderate middle class: The case of homeowners' resistance. *Asian Survey,* 45(5), 777–799.

Chan, CK-C (2012). Class or citizenship? Debating workplace conflict in China. *Journal of Contemporary Asia,* 42, 308–327.

Chan, CK-C and ES Hui (2012). The dynamics and dilemma of workplace trade union reform in China: The case of Honda workers's strike. *Journal of Industrial Relations,* 54(5), 653–668.

Chan, J (2009). Meaningful progress or illusory reform? Analyzing China's labor contract law. *New Labor Forum,* 18(2), 42–51.

Chan, J and N Pun (2010). Suicide as protest for the new generation of Chinese migrant workers: Foxconn, global capital, and the state. *The Asia-Pacific Journal,* 37, September 13.

Chan, KW (2003). Migration in China in the reform era: Characteristics, consequences, and implications. In *China's Developmental Miracle: Origins, Transformations, and Challenges,* AY So (ed.), pp. 111–135. Armonk, NY: M.E. Sharpe.

Chan, KW (2013). Cities of dreams. *South China Morning Post,* January 19, p. A15.

Chang, K-S (2003). Market socialism and ruralist welfare reform in post-socialist China. *Development and Society,* 32(2), 147–171.

Chang, K-S (2007). Developmental statism in the post-socialist context: China's reform politics through a Korean perspective. Paper presented to the conference Chinese Society and China Studies at Nanjing, May 26–27.

Chen, A (2002). Capitalist development, entrepreneurial class, and democratization in China. *Political Science Quarterly,* 117(3), 401–422.

Chen, F (2000). Subsistence crises, managerial corruption, and labor protests in China. *The China Journal,* 44, 41–63.

Chen, J and C Lu (2006). Does China's middle class think and act democratically? Attitudinal and behavioral orientations toward urban self-government. *Journal of Chinese Political Science*, 11(2), 1–20.

Chen, M (2011). *Tiger Girls: Women and Enterprises in China.* London: Routledge.

Chen, X (2005). *As Border Bend: Transnational Spaces on the Pacific Rim.* Lanham, MD: Rowman & Littlefield.

Cheng, JYS (2007). Introduction: Economic growth and new challenges. In *Challenges and Policy Programmes of China's New Leadership*, JYS Cheng (ed.), pp. 1–35. Hong Kong: City University of Hong Kong Press.

Cheng, T and M Selden (1994). The origins and social consequences of China's hukou system. *The China Quarterly*, 139, 644–668.

Chesneaux, J (1968). *The Chinese Labor Movement, 1919–1927.* Stanford: Stanford University Press.

CHINAdaily (2004). Middle class becomes rising power in China. *CHINAdaily*, November 6.

China Review News (2008). Zhang Yin proposes to eliminate the open-ended clause in the new labor contract law. *China Review News*, March 2. Available at http://www.chinareviewnews.com/doc/1005/8/1/3/100581306.html ?coluid=10&kindid=253&docid=100581306&mdate=0302092650. Accessed on May 26, 2013.

China Translated (2009). The black collar class. *China Translated*, June 11. Available at www.chinatranslated.com/?paged=19. Accessed on May 26, 2013.

Cohen, D (2013). China's superbank. *The Diplomat*, January 26.

Davis, DS (2000). Social class and transformation in urban China: Training, hiring, and promoting urban professionals and managers after 1949. *Modern China*, 26(3), 251–275.

Deng, Z and DJ Treiman (1997). The impact of the cultural revolution on trends in education attainment in the People's Republic of China. *American Journal of Sociology*, 103(2), 391–428.

Ding, X (1999). Who gets what, how? When Chinese state-owned enterprises become shareholding companies. *Problems of Post-Communism*, 46(3), 32–41.

Ding, X (2000a). Systemic irregularity and spontaneous property transformation in the Chinese financial system. *China Quarterly*, 163, 655–676.

Ding, X (2000b). The illicit asset stripping of Chinese state firms. *The China Journal*, 43, 1–28.

Dickson, BJ (2004). Beijing ambivalent reformers. *Current History*, 103(674), 249–255.

Django (2012). Wukan peasant victory sets stage for Chinese turmoil. *libcom.org*, January 9. Available at http://libcom.org/library/wukan-peasant-victory-sets-stage-chinese-turmoil [accessed on April 15, 2012].

Dong Fang Zao Bao (2005). Zhuan jia jian yan 3G pai zhao fa fang, jian yi yin wai zi yu min ying zi ben (Expert suggest to set up a 3G licence, to attract both foreign capital and local capital). Dong Fang Zao Bao, June 23. Available at http://www.chinabyte.com/telecom/201/2020701.shtml. Accessed on August 20, 2007.

Duckett, J (2001). Bureaucrats in business, Chinese style. *World Development*, 29, 23–37.

Eckholm, E (2001). Chinese officials order cities to bolster riot police forces. *New York Times*, January 30.

Economy, E (2005). China's environmental challenge. *Current History*, 104(683), 278–283.

Economy, E (2007). The great leap backward? The cost of China's environmental crisis. *Foreign Affairs*, 86(5), 82–85.

Edin, M (2003). State capacity and local agent control in China: CCP cadre management from a township perspective. *The China Quarterly*, 173, 35–42.

Evans, P (1995). *Embedded Autonomy: States and Industrial Transformation.* Princeton: Princeton University Press.

Feng, C (2012). Auspicious time for change in China. *The Financial Review*, October 13.

Ford, P (2010). Foreigners doing business in China feel boxed out: Report. *The Christian Science Monitor*, June 29.

Francis, C-B (2001). Quasi-public, quasi-private trends in emerging market economies: The case of China. *Comparative Politics*, 33, 275–294.

Friedman, E (2009). US and Chinese labour at a changing moment in the global neoliberal economy. *The Journal of Labor and Society*, 12(2), 219–234.

Friedman, E (2012). China in revolt. *Jocobin: A Magazine of Culture and Polemic*, No. 7–8. Available at http://jacobinmag.com/2012/08/china-in-revolt/. Accessed on May 26, 2013.

Friedman, E, P Pickowicz and M Selden (1991). *Chinese Village, Socialist State*. New Haven: Yale University Press.

Gallagher, ME (2002). Reform and openness: Why China's economic reforms have delayed democracy. *World Politics*, 54(3), 338–372.

Garcia, BC, M Chen and D Goodman (2011). New economic elites: The social basis of local power. Paper presented to the "Class and Class Consciousness in China" workshop at University of Sydney, January 31–February 2.

Garnaut, J (2013). Peoples' power will reform China, says Qin Xiao. *The Sydney Morning Herald*, January 8.

Gilboy, GJ and E Heginbotham (2004). The Latin Americanization of China? *Current History*, 103, 256–261.

Gobel, C and LH Ong (2012). *Social Unrest in China*. London: Europe China Research and Advice Network.

Gong, T (2006). Corruption and local governance: The double identity of Chinese local governments in market reform. *The Pacific Review*, 19(1), 85–102.

Goodman, D (1996). The People's Republic of China: The party-state, capitalist revolution and new entrepreneurs. In *The New Rich in Asia*, R Robison and DSG Goodman (eds.), pp. 225–242. London: Routledge.

Goodman, D (2000). Centre and periphery after twenty years of reform: Redefining the Chinese polity. Paper presented to the conference entitled "Centre-Periphery Relations in China", The Chinese University of Hong Kong, March 24–25.

Guan, X (2000). China's social policy: Reform and development in the context of marketization and globalization. *Social Policy and Administration*, 34, 115–130.

Guo, X (2001). Land expropriation and rural conflicts in China. *The China Quarterly*, 166, 422–439.

Guo, Y (2009). Farewell to class, except the middle class: The politics of class in contemporary China. *The Asia-Pacific Journal*, 26-2-09.

Hart-Landsberg, M and P Burkett (2004). China and socialism: Market reform and class struggle. *Monthly Review*, 56(3), 1–124.

Harvey, D (2005). *A Brief History of Neoliberalism*. New York: Oxford University Press.

He, Q (2000). China's listing social structure. *New Left Review*, 5, 69–99.

He, Q (2006). Officially sanctioned crime in China: A catalogue of lawlessness. *China Rights Forum*, No. 3.

He, Q (2009). The relationship between Chinese peasants' right to subsistence and China's social stability. *China Rights Forum*, No. 1.

Hinton, W (1998). The importance of land reform in the reconstruction of China. *Monthly Review*, 50(3), 147–160.

Hjellum, T (2000). Features of capitalism and the restructuring of ruling classes in China. *Copenhagen Journal of Asian Studies*, 14, 105–129.

Ho, P (2001). Who own China's land? *The China Quarterly*, 166, 394–421.

Hobsbawm, EJ (1997). *On History*. New York: The New Press.

Holz, C (2006). Why China's rise is sustainable? *Far Eastern Economic Review*, April, 41–47.

Howell, J (1998). An unholy trinity? Civil society, economic liberalization and democratization in post-Mao China. *Government and Opposition*, 33, 56–80.

Huang, Y (2013). In China, most politics is local. *The New York Times*, January 29.

Huchet, J-F (2000). Regional economies facing industrial restructuring: Towards new relationship between centre and local governments? Paper presented to the conference entitled "Centre–Periphery Relations in China", The Chinese University of Hong Kong, March 24–25.

Hui, ES and CK Chan (2011). The 'harmonious society' as a hegemonic project: Labour conflict and changing labour policies in China. *LABOUR, Capital and Society*, 44(2), 155–183.

Huntington, SP (1991). *The Third Wave: Democratization in the Late Twentieth Century*. Norman and London: University of Oklahoma Press.

Hussain, A (2005). Preparing China's social safety net. *Current History*, 104(683), 683–722.

Jiang, C (2010). Why foreign businesses in China are getting mad. *Time*, September 9.

Kahn, J (2006). A sharp debate erupt in China over ideologies. *New York Times*, March 12.

Kane, P (1988). *Famine in China, 1959-61: Demographic and Social Implications*. New York: St. Martin's Press.

Kennedy, S (2005). *The Business of Lobbying in China*. Cambridge: Harvard University Press.

Kerkvliet, BJT and M Selden (1998). Agrarian transformations in China and Vietnam. *The China Journal*, 40, 37–58.

Koo, H (1999). The middle classes in the East Asian newly industrializing societies: Issues, preliminary findings, and further questions. In *East Asian Middle Classes in Comparative Perspective*, Hsin-Huang Michael Hsiao (ed.), pp. 83–100. Academia Sinica: Institute of Ethnology.

Kraus, RC (1979). Withdrawal from the world-system: Self-reliance and class structure in China. In *The World-System of Capitalism: Past and Present*, W Goldfrank (ed.), pp. 237–259. Beverly Hills, CA: Sage Publications, Inc.

Kraus, RC (1981). *Class and Class Conflict in Chinese Socialism*. New York: Columbia University Press.

Kuhn, A (2004). A high price to pay for a job. *Far Eastern Economic Review*, 167(3), 30.

Lau, RWK (1997). China: Labour reform and the challenge facing the working class. *Capital and Race*, 61, 45–80.

Lau, M and CK Choi (2010). Hundreds clash as labour strife widens: Worker unrest spread to Yangtze river delta. *South China Morning Post*, LXVI(158), B1, A5.

Lee, C-K (1998). *Gender and the South China Miracle*. Berkeley: University of California Press.

Lee, C-K (2000). Pathways of labour insurgency. In *Chinese Society: Change, Conflict, and Resistance*, EJ Perry and M Selden (eds.), pp. 41–62. London and New York: Routledge.

Lee, C-K (2007). *Against the Law: Labor Protests in China's Rustbelt and Sunbelt*. Berkeley and Los Angeles: University of California Press.

Lee, CK and M Selden (2007). Durable inequality: The legacies of China's revolutions and the pitfalls of reform. In *Understanding Revolutions: Social Identities, Globalization and Modernity*, J Foran *et al.* (eds.). London: Routledge.

Lee, S-H *et al.* (1999). The impact of democratization on environmental movements. In *Asia's Environmental Movements: Comparative Perspective*, Y-S Lee and AY So (eds.), pp. 230–252. Armonk: M. E. Sharpe.

Lemos, G (2012). What keeps the Chinese up at night. *The New York Times*, September 9.

Leung, P (Unpublished). Leading strikes in the workshop of the world: Jewelry worker activists and the struggles of the new working class in China. PhD dissertation, Division of Social Science, Hong Kong University of Science and Technology.

Leung, P and AY So (2012). The making and re-making of the working class in South China. In *China's Peasants and Workers: Changing Class Identities*, B Carrillo and DSG Goodman (eds.), pp. 62–78. Cheltenham, UK: Edward Elgar.

Leung, P and AY So (2013). The new labor contract law in 2008: China's legal absorption of labor unrest. *Journal of Studies in Social Sciences*, 4(1), 131–160.

Li, C (2010). Introduction: The rise of the middle class in the middle kingdom. In *China's Emerging Middle Class*, C Li (ed.), pp. 3–31. Washington, DC: Brookings Institution Press.

Li, H (2003). Middle class: Friends or foes to Beijing's new leadership. *Journal of Chinese Political Science*, 8(1&2), 87–100.

Li, L (2002). Elections and popular resistance in rural China. *China Information*, 16(1), 89–107.

Liew, LH (2001). What is to be done? WTO, globalization and state–labour relations in China. *Australian Journal of Politics and History*, 47(1), 39–60.

Lin, J and X Sun (2010). Higher education expansion and China's middle class. In *China's Emerging Middle Class*, C Li (ed.), pp. 217–244. Washington, DC: Brookings Institution Press.

Lin, JY, R Tao and M Liu (2006). Decentralization and local governance in China's economic transition. In *Decentralization and Local Governance in Developing Countries*, P Bardhan and D Mookherjee (eds.), pp. 30–327. Cambridge: MIT Press.

Lin, S (2002). Too many fees and too many charges: China streamlines the fiscal system. In *China's Economy into the New Century*, J Wong and L Ding (eds.), pp. 182–192. Singapore: Singapore University Press.

Lipset, SM (1963). *Political Man*. Garden City, NY: Anchor.

Liu, I (1971). Make efforts to study amid the storm of class struggle. *Survey of China Mainland Magazines*, 1(715), 17.

Liu, M and J Ansfield (2007). Beijing's new deal. *Newsweek (Pacific Edition)*, 149(13), p. 26.

Liu, S (2009). The ordinary middle class in an ordinary community: The formation of the new middle class in China. Unpublished Dissertation, Department of Sociology, the Chinese University of Hong Kong.

Litzinger, R (2013). The labor question in China: Apple and beyond. *The South Atlantic Quarterly*, 112(1), 172–178.

Loo, B and SY Chow (2006). China's 1994 tax sharing reforms: One system, different impact. *Asian Survey*, 46, 215–237.

Lu, X and EJ Perry (eds.) (1997). *Danwei, the Changing Chinese Workplace in Historical and Comparative Perspective*. Armonk, NY: M.E. Sharpe.

Magdoff, H and JB Foster (2004). Editors' foreword to China and socialism. *Monthly Review*, 56(3), 2–6.

Mao, T-T (1967). *Selected Works of Mao Tse-Tung. Vol. II.* Beijing: Foreign Language Press.

Mao, T-T (1972). *Quotations from Chairman Mao Tsetung.* Beijing: Foreign Language Press.

Meisner, M (1999). *Mao's China and After.* New York: The Free Press.

Montaperto, RN (1972). From revolutionary successors to revolutionaries: Chinese students in the early stages of the cultural revolution. In *Elites in the People's Republic of China*, RA Scalapino (ed.), pp. 592–593. Seattle: University of Washington Press.

Moore, B Jr (1966). *Social Origins of Dictatorship and Democracy.* Penguin.

Morrison, WM (2009). China and the global financial crisis: Implications for the United States. Washington: Congressional Research Service, CRS Report for Congress.

Nan Fang Du Shi Bao (Southern City News) (2003). Guang dong gao pei ban tou shi: Wu nian hua yi yi, guan yuan yang jin xiu. *Nan Fang Du Shi Bao* (Southern City News), August 30.

Nanping Shi (2004). *Nanping Jiao Yu Ju Dui Fa Zhan Jiao Shi Dang Yuan De Diao Cha Yu Si Kao* (Nanping City Education Bureau's Survey and Rethinking on the Prospect of Recruiting Teachers into the Party), June 28. Available at http://www.npjy.com/newsInfo.aspx?pkId=495017. Accessed on May 26, 2013.

Naughton, B (2007). The assertive center: Beijing moves against local government control of land. *China Leadership Monitor*, No. 20.

Nee, V (1989). A theory of market transition. *American Sociological Review*, 54, 663–681.

Nee, V (2000). The role of the state in making markets. *Journal of Institutional and Theoretical Economics*, 156, 64–88.

Ni, C-C (2001). Communists at ironic juncture. *LA Times*, July 3.

Nolan, P (2004). *China at the Crossroads*. Cambridge: Polity.

Nonini, DM (2008). Is China becoming neoliberal? *Critique of Anthropology*, 28(2), 145–176.

O'Brien, KJ (2004). Neither transgressive nor contained: Boundary-spanning contention in China. In *State and Society in 21st Century China*, PH Gries and S Rosen (eds.), pp. 105–122. New York: Routledge Curzon.

O'Brien, KJ (2009). Rural protest. *Journal of Democracy*, 20(3), 25–28.

O'Brien, K and L Li (2006). *Right Resistance in China*. Cambridge: Cambridge University Press.

Oi, J (1989). *State and Peasant in Contemporary China*. Berkeley: University of California Press.

Oi, J (1992). Fiscal reform and the economic foundations of local state corporatism in China. *World Politics*, 45, 99–126.

Oi, J (1995). The role of the local state in China's transitional economy. *China Quarterly*, 144, 1132–1149.

Ogden, S (2003). Chinese nationalism: The precedence of community and identity over individual rights. In *China's Developmental Miracle: Origins, Transformations, and Challenges*, AY So (ed.), pp. 224–245. Armonk, NY: M.E. Sharpe.

Orlik, T (2011). Unrest grows as economy booms. *Wall Street Journal*, September 26. Available at http://online.wsj.com/article/SB10001424 053111903703604576587070600504108.html [accessed on April 15, 2012].

Page, J (2011). Wave of unrest rocks China. *Wall Street Journal*, June 14. Available at http://online.wsj.com/article/SB10001424052702304665 90457638314290723 2726.html [accessed on April 15, 2012].

Parish, WL and E Michelson (1996). Politics and markets: Dual transformations. *American Journal of Sociology*, 101, 1042–1059.

Pearson, M (1998). China's emerging business class: Democracy's harbinger. *Current History*, 97, 268–272.

Perry, E (2007). Studying Chinese politics: Farewell to revolution? *The China Journal*, 57, 1–22.

Perry, E and M Selden (2000). Introduction: Reform and resistance in contemporary China. In *Chinese Society: Change, Conflict, and Resistance*,

P Elizabeth and M Selden (eds.), pp. 1–20. London and New York: Routledge.

Petras, J (2006). Past, present and future of China: From semi-colony to world power? *Journal of Contemporary Asia*, 36(4), 423–441.

Phoenix TV (2006). China's middle class: Reality or illusion. *Phoenix TV*, July 17, 2006.

Pogrebin, R (2011). China's new cultural revolution: A surge in art collecting. *The New York Times*, September 6, 2011.

Pomfret, J (2001). China allows its capitalist to join party: Communists recognize rise of private business. Washington Post Foreign Service, July 2, p. A01. Available at http://www.washingtonpost.com.

Pringle, T (2002). Industrial unrest in China — A labour movement in the making? *China Labour Bulletin*, January 31. Available at http://www.hartford-hwp.com/archives/55/294.html [accessed on April 13, 2003].

Pun, N (1999). Becoming Dagongmei: The politics of identity and difference in reform China. *China Journal*, 42, 1–19.

Pun, N (2001). Cultural construction of labor politics: Gender, kinship, and ethnicity in a Shenzhen workplace. In *The Chinese Triangle of Mainland-Taiwan-Hong Kong: Comparative and Institutional Analyses*, AY So *et al.* (eds.), pp. 103–116. Westport, CT: Greenwood Press.

Pun, N and CK Chan (2008). The subsumption of class discourse in China. *Boundary 2*, 35(2), 75–91.

Ramzy, A (2008). A new call for Chinese democracy. *Times*, December 10.

Renmin Ribao (1968). Never forget class struggle. *Renmin Ribao*, April 23, p. 4.

Roberts, D and J Zhao (2011). China's super-rich buy a better life abroad. *Bloomberg Business Week*, November 22. Available at http://www.businessweek.com/magazine/chinas-superrich-buy-a-better-life-abroad-11222011.html [accessed on April 15, 2012].

Robinson, J (1970). *The Cultural Revolution in China*. Harmondsworth: Penguin.

Roubini, N (2008). The rising risk of hard landing in China. *Japan Focus*, November 4.

Saich, T (2007). Focus on social development. *Asian Survey*, 47, 32–43.

Sheridan, M (2009). China's hidden unrest as boom ends; with joblessness soaring, Michael Sheridan reveals the scale of the protests the state media ignore. *The Sunday Times*, February 1, p. 18.

Shirk, SL (1982). *Competitive Comrades: Career Incentives and Student Strategies in China*. Berkeley and Los Angeles: University of California Press.

Shu, X (2013). Dim hopes for a free press in China. *The New York Times*, January 14.

Shue, V (2004). Legitimacy crisis in China? In *State and Society in 21st Century China*, PH Gries and S Rosen (eds.), pp. 24–49. New York: RoutledgeCurzon.

Silver, BJ and G Arrighi (2000). Workers north and south. In *2001 Socialist Register: Working Classes, Global Realities*, L Panitch and C Leys (eds.). New York: Monthly Review Press.

So, AY (2007). The state and labor insurgency in post-socialist China: Implication for development. In *Challenges and Policy Programmes of China's New Leadership*, JYS Cheng (ed.), pp. 133–151. Hong Kong: City University of Hong Kong press.

So, AY (2010a). Post-socialist state, transnational corporations, and the battle for labor rights in China at the turn of the 21st century. *Development and Society*, 39, 97–118.

So, AY (2010b). Globalization and China: From neoliberal capitalism to state developmentalism in East Asia. In *Globalization in the 21st Century: Labor, Capital, and the State on a World Scale*, B Berberoglu (ed.), pp. 133–154. New York: Macmillan Palgrave.

So, AY (2012). Global capitalist crisis and the rise of China to the world scene. In *Beyond the Global Capitalist Crisis: The World Economy in Transition*, B Berberoglu (ed.), pp. 123–144. Surrey: Ashgate.

So, AY and C Chu (2012). The transition from neoliberalism to state neoliberalism in China at the turn of the twenty-first century. In *Developmental Politics in Transition: The Neoliberal Era and Beyond*, K-S Chang, B Fine and L Weiss (eds.), pp. 166–187. New York: Palgrave Macmillan.

So, AY and M Hikam (1989). Class in the writings of Wallerstein and Thompson: Toward a class struggle analysis. *Sociological Perspectives*, 32(4), 453–467.

So, AY and S Hua (1992). Democracy as an antisystemic movement in Taiwan, Hong Kong, and China: A world system analysis. *Sociological Perspectives*, 35(2), 385–404.

So, AY and Suwarsono (1990). Class theory or class analysis? A reexamination of the Marx's unfinished chapter on class. *Critical Sociology*, 17(2), 35–55.

So, BWY (2005). Privatization. In *Critical Issues in Contemporary China*, C Tubilewicz (ed.), pp. 49–78. New York and London: Routledge.

Szelenyi, I (2008). A theory of transition. *Modern China*, 34, 165–175.

Solinger, DJ (1992). Urban entrepreneurs and the state: The merger of state and society. In *State and Society in China*, A Rosenbaum (ed.), pp. 121–142. Boulder: Westview.

Tang, M, D Wood and J Zhao (2009). The attitudes of the Chinese middle class towards democracy. *Journal of Chinese Political Science*, 14, 81–95.

Tang, W-S and H Chung (2002). Rural–urban transition in China: Illegal land use and construction. *Asia Pacific Viewpoint*, 43(1), 43–62.

Tanner, MS (2005). *Chinese Government Responses to Rising Social Unrest*. Testimony presented to the US–China economic and security review commission, April 14. Santa Monica: RAND Corporation.

Taubmann, W (2000). Urban administration, urban development, and migrant enclaves. Paper presented to the "International Workshop on Resource Management, Urbanization, and Governance in Hong Kong and the Zhujiang Delta", The Chinese University of Hong Kong, May 23–24.

Taylor, B and I Li (2007). Is the ACFTU a union and does it matter? *Journal of Industrial Relations*, 49, 701–715.

The Economist (2002). To get rich is glorious. *The Economist,* January 19.

The Economist (2006). Asia: Dreaming of harmony; China. *The Economist,* October 21.

The Economist (2007). Rural unrest in China. *Economist.com/Global China,* March 15.

The Editorial Board (2013). China's communist inheritance: A ticket to wealth. *The Washington Post,* January 4.

Thompson, EP (1978). Eighteenth-century english society: Class struggle without class? *Social History*, 4, 133–165.

Thornton, P (2004). Comrades and collectives in arms: Tax resistance, evasion, and avoidance strategies in post-Mao China. In *State and Society in 21ˢᵗ-Century China*, PH Gries and S Rosen (eds.), pp. 87–104. New York and London: RoutledgeCurzon.

Tomba, L (2010). The housing effect: The making of China's social distinctions. In *China's Emerging Middle Class*, C Li (ed.), pp. 193–216. Washington, DC: Brookings Institution Press.

Tsai, KS (2005). Capitalists without a class: Political diversity among private entrepreneurs in China. *Comparative Political Studies*, 38(9), 1130–1158.

UNDP (2006). UNDP China wins 2006 poverty eradication awards. Available at http://www.undp.org/poverty/stories/pov-award06-china.htm [accessed on January 10, 2009].

Unger, J (2006). China's conservative middle class. *Far Eastern Economic Review*, April, 27–31.

Walder, AG (1984). The remaking of the Chinese working class, 1949–1981. *Modern China*, 10(1), 3–48.

Walder, AG (1986). *Communist Neo-Traditionalism: Work and Authority in Chinese Industry.* Berkeley and Los Angeles: University of California Press.

Walder, AG (1996). Markets and inequalities in transitional economies: Toward testable theories. *American Journal of Sociology*, 101, 1060–1073.

Walder, AG (1997). Does China face an unstable future? In *China Review 1997*, M Brosseau, K Hsin-chi and YY Kueh (eds.), pp. 344–345. Hong Kong: Chinese University Press.

Wallerstein, I (1979). *The Capitalist World-Economy.* Cambridge: Cambridge University Press.

Wallerstein, I (1984). *The Politics of the Capitalist World-Economy.* Cambridge: Cambridge University Press.

Wallerstein, I (2010). How to think about China. *Commentary*, Fernand Braudel Center, Binghamton University, No. 273, January 15, 1–2. Available at http://fbc.binghamton.edu/eng2010.htm [accessed on February 7, 2010].

Walker, KLM (2006). Gangster capitalism and peasant protest in China: The last twenty years. *The Journal of Peasant Studies*, 33(1), 1–33.

Walker, KLM (2008). From covert to overt: Everyday peasant politics in China and the implications for transnational agrarian movements. *Journal of Agrarian Change*, 8(2–3), 482–488.

Wang, F (2008). *Boundaries and Categories: Rising Inequality in Post-Socialist Urban China.* Stanford: Stanford University Press.

Wang, H, RP Appelbaum, F Deguili and N Lichtenstein (2009). China's new labour contract law: Is China moving towards increased power for workers? *Third World Quarterly*, 30(3), 485–501.

Wang, S and A Hu (1999). *The Political Economy of Uneven Development: The Case of China.* Armonk: M.E. Sharpe.

Wang, S and A Hu (2001). *The Chinese Economy in Crisis: State Capacity and Tax Reform.* Armonk, NY: M. E. Sharpe.

Wank, D (1995). Private business, bureaucracy, and political alliance in a Chinese city. *Australian Journal of Chinese Affairs,* 33, 55–71.

Wassener, B (2012). Manufacturing in China slows further. *The New York Times,* August 23.

Watson, JL (1984). Introduction: Class and class formation in Chinese society. In *Stratification in Post-Revolutionary China,* JL Watson (ed.), pp. 1–15. Cambridge: Cambridge University Press.

Wedman, A (2000). Budgets, extra-budgets, and small treasures: Illegal monies and local autonomy in China. *Journal of Contemporary China,* 9(25), 489–511.

Wen, T (2001). Centenary reflections on the 'three dimensional problem' of rural China. *Inter-Asia Cultural Studies,* 2(2), 287–295.

Wen, T *et al.* (2012). Ecological civilization, indigeneous culture, and rural reconstruction in China. *Monthly Review,* 64(7), 29–35.

White, G, J Howell and X Shang (1996). *In Search of Civil Society.* Oxford: Clarendon Press.

Whyte, MK (2010). *Myth of the Social Volcano: Perception of Inequality and Distributive Justice in Contemporary China.* Stanford: Stanford University Press.

Wines, M (2010a). China fortifies state businesses to fuel growth. *The New York Times,* August 29.

Wines, M (2010b). As China rises, fears grow on whether boom can endure. *The New York Times,* January 12.

Wines, M (2012). A populists downfall exposes ideological divisions in China's ruling party. *The New York Times,* April 6.

Wong, E (2013). In China, widening discontent among the communist party faithful. *The New York Times,* January 19.

World Bank (2012). *China 2030: Building a Modern, Harmonious, and Creative High-Income Society.* Washington, DC: The World Bank and Development Research Council of the State Council, the People's Republic of China.

World by Data (2007). Thousands of nine dragon workers went on strike. Zhang Yin accused labor contract law has hindered the development of enterprises. *World by Data*, December 14. Available at http://news. worldbydata.com/zxnewview-26540.htm. Accessed on May 26, 2013.

Wortzel, LM (1987). *Class in China: Stratification in a Classless Society.* New York: Greenwood.

Wu, J-M (2001). State policy and Guanxi network adaptation in China: Local bureaucratic rent-seeking. *Issues and Studies*, 37(1), 20–48.

Wu, Y (2007). Yesterday's class enemies: Class ideology and politics of the cultural revolution. *China Study Group*, May 23.

Yep, R (2007). Tax assignment reform and its impact on county finance: Enhancing regulatory capacity for the central state? Paper presented to the International Conference on "State Capacity of China in the 21st century", City University of Hong Kong, April 19–20.

Yu, J (2004). A single spark starts a prairie fire. *New Internationalist*, No. 371.

Yu, J (2008). Emerging trends in violent riots. *China Security*, Summer, 75–76.

Yu, J (2010). Yu Jianrong on maintaining a baseline of social stability. *China Studies Group*, April 3.

Zhang, L (2010). *In Search of Paradise. Middle Class Living in a Chinese Metropolis.* Ithaca, NY: Cornell University Press.

Zhang, QF and JA Donaldson (2008). The rise of agrarian capitalism with Chinese characteristics: Agricultural modernization, agribusiness, and collective land rights. *The China Journal*, 60, 25–47.

Zhao, Y (2012). The struggle for socialism in China: The Bo Xilai sage and beyond. *Monthly Review*, 64(5), 1–17.

Zheng, Y (2004). *Globalization and State Transformation in China.* New York: Cambridge University Press.

Zhou, K (1996). *How the Farmers Changed China: Power of the People.* Boulder: Westview Press.

Zweig, D (1997). Rural people, the politicians, and power. *The China Journal*, 38, 153–168.

INDEX